additional comments on

Journey to the Ancestral Self

An inspiration. . . . It awoke in me a yearning to search for my own cultural and spiritual being that has been denied for so long.

Fay Mosley
Director of the Gandangara Local Aboriginal Land Council,
Liverpool, Australia

Gems of wisdom and keen observations. . . . His view compares with the ancient Buddhist concept of the dependent co-arising of all that is.

Rhoda Gilman
Minnesota History Magazine

A landmark work of its kind.

Keewaydinoquay
Mashikikwe of the Chippewa Tribe

JOURNEY TO THE ANCESTRAL SELF

TAMARACK SONG

The Native Lifeway Guide to
Living in Harmony with Earth Mother
BOOK 1

STATION HILL PRESS

Published by Station Hill Press, Inc. Barrytwon, New York, 12507.

Pen and ink drawings © 1994 Francene Hart.

Text and cover design by Susan Qasha, assisted by Anastasia McGee, Dominick Amarante, and Vicki Hickman.

Library of Congress Cataloging-in-Publication Data

Song, Tamarack, 1948-
  Journey to the ancestral self : the native lifeway guide to living in harmony with the Earth Mother / Tamarack Song.
    p. cm.
ISBN 0-88268-178-8 (v. 1) : $14.95
  1. Spiritual life. 2. Earth—Religious aspects. 3. Indians of North America—Religion—Miscellanea. I. Title.
BL624.S653 1994
299'.7—dc20   94-7307
                                        CIP

Manufactured in the United States of America.

Some of my earliest memories are of the little pink porcelain cup Mom gave me for picking wild Strawberries with her, and of the Willow bush whose branch she used in showing me how to make whistles. On walks to the mailbox, she'd name for me the prairie flowers that lapped the road.

She was my first wild foods instructor. After showing me how to gather wild fruits, she'd let me boil them down on an open Fire in the backyard before she converted them into more formal delicacies. She admonished me for the first bird I killed, prompting me to look at life in a different way.

Even though I didn't always have her approval for my adventures, I always had—and have—her love and support.

Acknowledgements

This book was written on the backs of matchbooks, on the back of my hand, on napkins, and on bark strips—anything handy when the words came. The damp blade of a Canoe paddle was often my desk. That, combined with the fact that I don't type (and refuse to learn), made the compilation of this manuscript a task demanding more than just genius. The polish and form of that which you are holding is the result of the toil and conviction of the woman I once walked with, Zhingakwe, Medicine Fir Tree Woman of the Dodem Turtle.

George Burnett's commitment, orderly thinking, and knack for editing made it possible for this book to be completed weeks rather than months past deadline. I am deeply grateful for his help.

Contents

List of Charts

I

Finding the Trail

She took my hand and I became with her
as I became with the Storm and the Lake and the Sand at my feet.

Introduction to the Series

Work was so hot that a beer might almost taste good—or so went that particular excuse for a stop at the East Side Pub. I knew suffering through another gassy brew wouldn't bring me a warm touch and the meaning of life, yet I had to give those glitzy commercial promises a chance. Marriage didn't do it, nor did a second stab at college.

Now I was stuck in a business so debilitating that it made my recent Vietnam War hassles look good.

I eased in the door, no doubt wearing a frown influenced by the sting of air sharp with smoke, stale beer, and urine. She was alone at the first table, and a stranger, yet she gestured for me to join her as if expecting me. She wore a faint smile that spelled recognition . . . and invitation.

I never met a Sage, yet I sensed that this calm, deep-eyed woman was one. After I ordered a drink, she said in a coppery voice that they called her "She Who Talks With Loons." I didn't bother to introduce myself—I couldn't. In fact I had trouble saying anything.

So there I was, in a dingy tavern, entranced by a woman whose mystic words drew me into a time and a land that I thought no longer existed. I never finished my drink.

The next morning she took me north in her aged Volkswagen bus. It was hot and the road was rutted, dusty, and long. We talked but I can't remember a word of what was said. All I recall is her ethereal image illumined yellow by the Sun. And her hint of a smile, which floated as lightly over everything she said as did her lacy hair in the breeze of the open window.

As we walked up the sun-speckled path to the big log Cabin, I felt I was approaching a Cathedral in the Pines. The musty interior and smell of times old and unfamiliar sent a chill to my bones. Hanging in the timbered expanse of the ceiling were pack baskets, bark trays, and traps. On high shelves were bundles and sacks of goods that wore cloaks of aged dust and bore the stains of essences that time had leached out of their unknown contents.

While I absorbed myself in the Cabin's patina, Talks With Loons told me about the Cabin's origins and past life: It was built late in the last century by her ancestors as a trading post. The site was at the confluence of several lake country trails—already a place of gathering and barter. The far-ranging People who came there to trade often stayed for periods of time, the Cabin becoming a receptacle for their dying lifeway.

That night as my gaze lost itself in the rafters of the Cabin, I sensed things moving about its lofty expanse—living things that I couldn't quite make out with my eyes. But the dust lay as undisturbed as ever. That spine-tingling feeling returned. The night was stormy; I reasoned that perhaps the Wind in the shakes and the Thunder and Lightning distorting the whine and glow of the lamp were playing with my imagination.

Then the Thunder beckoned and the Lightning illumined the bending Trees that were motioning for us to come out to the shore of the Lake behind the Cabin. Without speaking, we each slipped off our clothes and went out to join the Rage. Then I felt and recognized them—the Old Ones who lived with their artifacts in the rafters. They came out with us.

Lake and Sky lost their distinction as the pained Wind boiled the Water and forced the gushing Rain into it. Slapped with the shivering fury, Trees crackled and hissed, and my eyes and skin winced in involuntary defiance. The scene was given an eerie infusion by the stark blue-white of the constant Lightning.

I glanced at Talks With Loons; she glowed in the same hue as the Lightning and her eyes took on the deep, hot orange of those of her namesake. That frightful instant bulged my eyes and grabbed my breath in the sudden awareness that our meeting must be for a purpose. Stunned and overwhelmed, I dared not look at her again.

She took my hand, and I became with her as I became with the Storm and the Lake and the Sand at my feet. I was nothing; the Rain passed through me and the Wind felt no resistance from my chest. I was cold—as cold as the Rain, but I wasn't there to shiver. I was frightened—as frightened as the elements were furious—but I had no form to cower or flinch. I was nothing but the scream and pulse of the Storm; all I felt was an awareness that I somehow existed in that dimensionless expanse where Wind and Light and Water came together. The Old Ones were there, dancing. They danced through me, because I was nothing.

That night, as I was lost to drained, numb sleep, Talks With Loons did a portrait of a Wolf. In deja vu, I sometimes look into those Wolf eyes and again dwell where the Old Ones dance, where that Storm still rages. And to some few who see that Wolf, the Storm blows through them as it blew through me. It has drawn them into those eyes, into the skull of that Wolf, and they have seen through those eyes what a Wolf sees, as all Wolves live in the Dance.

A week later, she gave me another drawing. I didn't tell her what I saw and felt in that Storm, but there it was on paper before me. No one sees that drawing, because each person has to see it on her own calling, in her own dimension, within her own Vision.

Talks With Loons and I don't talk much when we're together. She is not a teacher or an example for me, but a mirror. She initiated my Journey. She gave me the Gift of Being Nothing. And she asked that I let the Voice of the Cabin dwell within me and flow through me. That's it; after that first day I never saw the Cabin again, she never mentions what transpired there, and we've never since had a similar experience together. Since then,

I see her, or she sees me, when I need a mirror. Sometimes I'm the buffoon, sometimes I'm the hothead, sometimes I'm lost in myself, but always she's Raven—the reflector of my own questions and blunders and squinted vision.

Because of the Power of Talks with Loons' respectful presence, you'll know her better than you'll know me when you and I finish Walking together in these books. Perhaps she'll Walk on with you.

Tamarack Song,	*Mashkigwateg w Nagamon,*
Owl Clan	*Gookookoo Dodem*
Headwaters Wilderness	*Ogidadjiwani Bagwaj*
Blueberry Moon,	*Miinan Gissis,*
Year of the Summer Frosts	*Gaa Takiniibing*

For the Deer and the Grasses I have written this book,
so that we can again be At One with them.

These Books . . .

. . . are a Journey. Deep within each of us is a person who dances to the Drum around the ritual Fire, a person who knows healing lore from times when plants spoke, a person who yearns for the peace and Blessings of walking again in the Balance of Our Earth—Our Mother.

This Journey will bring us to the Voice of our own blood Ancestors from the time before time was kept. It will give us invisibility; it will give the grace of a ballerina to our walk and the fleetness of Dolphin to our swim; it will give us the Personal Power we now have but can't use. It will give us back our home and reintroduce us to Our Mother.

These books have no beginning. They are a glance at the flow and rhythm that brings past to future by being in the fullness of the moment. In the same way, these books have no end. The ends of the sentences are not for us, nor are the ends of the chapters or the ends of the books. In the hollows of these words and the times after these periods, the Song of our Ancestors will be heard. When it happens, put the books down and listen. It is precious time with the Elders, time we have been too long without. It is our birthright. It is also our sacred duty, as heir to our family's Memories. The books will be there when we return; don't let them get in the way of their reason for being before us.

There is nothing new in these books. Many things may at first sound new to us, but we will soon discover that we already know them, or that we can read them on pages ever before us. They are locked in our Ancestral Memory; they are on the tip of Squirrel's tongue outside our window; they are being whispered for us to hear right at this moment. These books are a collection of keys that will unlock those sources for us. Once the keys become part of us, we won't need these (or any other) books anymore.

In this book there are exercises to help us grow in awareness and attune our senses and intuitions. They lead to skills in the following books that will allow us to partake in the Blessings of Walking the Old Way—the lifeway common to the natural realm. We'll learn how to draw the spirit of Fire from wood, how to befriend Mosquitos, how to touch a Deer, how to speak the language that travels beneath words. We'll learn these things not as isolated skills, but as incidentals to the Path of Balance.

My first inclination is to ask you not to read these books. Knowledge is well conveyed by books, but wisdom shies from words not filled with the breath of life. Printed words risk being static and are prone to misinterpretation. They are woefully inadequate in sharing that which is not bounded by time and space. And I am bound by trust and greater wisdom to share some things only in their own time, only in a sacred manner, and only as people are prepared for them. So there will be times when you need wizened guidance, and these books will fail you.

If you can, take this Journey with the assistance of a Guide. Seek out the Elders in your area; you'll recognize them as the ones who live what they believe, and who guide you to seek your own Voice and Vision rather than having you adopt theirs. Empty your cup before you go (as a full one has no room), and a true Elder will likely not refuse you.

These books are best utilized as adjuncts to having a Guide, so Part I of these books is devoted to the Guide-Seeker relationship. Even so, I know that many of you are isolated and will still walk alone with these words. For you, I wish to say that these words will sometimes become transparent, and what you need may appear through them.

I have written these books in part because the Journey to self-discovery and Vision is a Path that is shrouded in the shame and denial of the dominant culture. Vestiges of the Old Way that survive in that culture are either shallowed by tinsel or dangled before us as a mythic reward. "Know thyself" is the directive given by People of Spirit in every age and tradition. When we know who we are—when these books become a cliché to our existence—we'll reapproach that culture with a temperance and a benevolence that will speak to others, whether that be our conscious intent or not. Just by being ourselves—our intrinsic selves—we'll ease for others the Journey to self.

Some of us have already reached a place where the placebos of the culture have lost their magic and the Voices shout from deep within to be heard. For those amongst us, I have especially written these books.

I know of too few books and too few teachers who are applying the wisdoms of the Old Way to today. Some advocate the return of yesterday, and many, emerging from generations of cultural stew, unwittingly share their hybrid traditions as the Old Way. Some give us the allegorical jingles and feathers to dance in; few give us the marrow and guts we need Walk with.

In these final days, Our Mother asks us to return to Her, to respect and care for Her, in the way that gives Her Honor. We've tried many other "new, improved" ways, which invariably devour each other or choke on their own corpulence. I'm walking beside you in these pages as we relearn the Way that transcends the vagaries of time and notion.

For the Deer and the Grasses I have written these books, so that we can again be At One with them. As importantly, I wish these books to help us be At One with our own species. As Deer lick each others' coats and Grasses sway together in the breezes, so also do we need to learn again how to trust and cherish and nurture those of our own Blood. By finding ourselves, we also find the self in others; by touching the Power and beauty in others, we also touch the Power and beauty in ourselves. We all dance and cry and thirst the same things; it is the Song of our species. We are but fingers on the same hand, as the same Blood, the same Memory, the same Spirit flows in all of us. In our neighbor is our heart, our eyes; in her steps we also Walk, in her breath we also find life. In the quest of self, we find the Path of our species.

My dilemma in writing of matters sacred is to give it a life that will bridge our lack of common cultural soil and shared spiritual Blood. I cover some things that would not be discussed amongst Native Peoples, either because they are already understood as part of the cultural context, or because they are considered unmentionable. Talk of an individual's spiritual realm would be embarrassing and disrespectful, as well as an infringement—and possibly a negation—of that person's Power.

In sharing some of my own spiritual experiences, I break with that tradition. The Spirit-realm does not exist in a general or abstract form; it exists for each of us only as we give it breath. So I have chosen to root my sharing in the tracks of my own Path. This is the only way I can give you living words.

We are each given Gifts and Powers that are intended only for us. In speaking them we risk losing them by giving them away. So I have been cautious to relate my Dreams and Visions in a way that will not release their Gifts. They are like good wine that will keep indefinitely in a cool, dark cellar but will deteriorate quickly when brought up to the warmth and light. I am trustful that what I have given here of my Spirit-Way will be given back to me.

There is little ceremony or ritual in these books, as they are about those things from which ceremonies flow. The outward expression of spirit is personal to each of us and can sometimes be shared when people of like spirit come together. Spontaneous or ritualized ceremony gives Honor to The Mother, and Power to the participants, because it draws its breath from within each person participating. Ceremony that is imposed or followed without heart is hollow and debilitating.

One of the incentives for these books was my experience with hollow rituals and traditions gone stale. Many times have I been expected to participate in a ceremony in body without concern for my involvement in spirit. And many times have I been left feeling like a spoke in a wheel that doesn't know why it is turning.

Our culture did not grace us with ceremonies, because it shares no spirit to ceremonialize; it gave us only relic traditions because living traditions interfere with expediency and its pragmatic ways. So our thirst drives us to adopt tradition for the sake of tradition, to dogmatically practice a prescribed ritual in hopes that it will spark an upwelling of the sacred within us.

I own nothing and will receive no recompense for these books. If their breath fans the ember of our smouldering spirit to visibly glow in its expression of Blessings and Balance, I will be honored enough for having written them.

Because of the great diversity of Native Lifeways, I run the risk of over-generalizing when I speak of the Old Way as common to all Native Peoples. For example, the Native North Americans cannot be said to share a spirituality, because there are as many differences amongst them as there are amongst the major religions of the world. My focus in these texts is not on the peculiarities that distinguish people, but on the underlying threads that show them as kin.

You and I would describe the same Tree differently if we came upon it from different directions, at different times, in different seasons. In the same way these will be books of fact for you only in that area where my reality meshes with yours. For me, these are entirely books of fact, because they are a reflection of my personal reality. Your eyes, your heart, are not mine, so I do not ask you to, nor will I be offended when you do not, accept all of my reality as yours.

I regret that I'm not able to share with each of you personally, individually, as there are many things that can only be shared on a one-to-one basis. However, my regret is not for loss to you, because I know these things are available to you elsewhere and will come to you as you seek and need them on your Journey.

These books will only open doors; it is for each of us to walk beyond the doors. They are like a roadsign, like a directional arrow; they are not a Path themselves, not your Path or my Path. If we grasp the spirit of these books, we will leave them with more questions than answers; if they grasp our spirit, they will leave us with the tools to find those answers.

...and How to Use Them

A book of spiritual teachings that does not contain the tools for applying those teachings would do better service as the Tree from which it came. The tools and the teachings are as inseparable from one another, and as needed by one another, as our vision needs our eyes.

These books are mated in the same way; they are as textbooks to workbooks. Together they address the dual personalities—ethereal and physical, dream and craft, inner realm and Greater Circle. Although any of these books will stand alone as an insightful Journey into the realms it explores, progressing in the books simultaneously will bring us a greater Balance.

These books are written to be reread, as they do not speak all they have to say on first acquaintance. If that were the case, much would be lost, because we can only receive that which we are ready for. As we progress on our Path, these books will likely guide us to deeper awarenesses and higher levels of skill than we thought possible the last time we read them. So travel lightly and slowly with them, taking what they have to give without force or frustration. Patience and Respect open all doors.

Besides guiding the steps on our Journey, these books are intended as reference works. We can keep them handy for a ready check on skills, techniques, and exercises, and perhaps for when a kindly friend is needed to help wade confusion.

I have taken some license with words, with grammar, and with the language in general, in order to surmount some of their limitations. For instance, some words are capitalized to indicate a deeper significance than is typically associated with them (such as *Vision*, which in these texts refers to the Lifepath a person seeks through a period of Fasting and isolation). The names of animals and plants are capitalized to indicate that all of life is sacred. Words are fabricated and sentence structures are juggled where our language gives us no parallel with Native expression. *She* and *he* are used interchangeably as generic pronouns, to give Honor to both sexes. Old and archaic words (such as *wizened*, defined here as *venerable, insightful*) and phrasings appear, partly to bring the reader into the realm of the text (in the way that "hallowed be thy name" elicits a different feeling than "your name is holy"), and partly because of the influence of old books on my writing style. Other aberrations will be self-evident.

The index is the web whose strands keep us in touch with topics that span more than one chapter. Some meanings will unfold as we progress through the book; the index will help us to backtrack so that we can easily revisit the steps in that unfoldment. The index is also a quick way to take advantage of the relatedness of all the books.

As we will discover on into this Journey, we retain more, and in different ways, when we hear something rather than read it. We are given even more if we can both hear and read it. In Honor of this, I have voice recorded these books and it is available on cassette tape. For many, the most empowering way to Walk this Journey will be to listen to the recording while reading along in the book.

At the end of some chapters are suggested readings, which are listed under the honorable heading of *Elder*. Most of them give added voice to enrich the chorus; a couple of them have contrary voices that disrupt the chorus and force us to arrange our own harmony. Books have become our Elders; much of the wisdoms of the Old Way would not be available to us were it not recorded before the Old Ones left us. I hold several of these books in high regard. Because the spirits of their sources live on within them, the Elders can again sit amongst us.

My focus in these texts is not on the peculiarities that distinguish people, but on the underlying threads that show them as kin.

They teach language — mostly the language
of Conquerors/Exploiters, seldom the language of Wolf and Wind.

Seeking Wisdom: The Guide as Raven

Our Dilemma

They dragged me into kindergarten kicking and screaming; they dragged me into first grade kicking and screaming. After that, they had me broken to the point where I'd sit and go through the motions, but they never did get me to fully participate. I grew frustrated and displeased with myself, because I didn't fit there, yet I had no idea where I did fit.

We are on a Journey to know ourselves. The first step is the most demanding, and often the most frustrating, because we don't know what we're looking for. Once found, the sense of self and the Personal Power it engenders makes it easy to become that person. Unfortunately, it also makes it easy to deny that person. The unknown cannot be suppressed; the known can.

The dominant culture feeds on people who have given up (or not discovered) their Personal Power and who have acquiesced to another's. The belts and gears of this giant culture-machine would stop cold if we each began to listen to our hearts. Life as we know it would become life as we dream it.

But they can only allow us to dream; they can't afford to have us follow our Dreams. We are given no support, no encouragement, to be ourselves. Therapy, ostracization, and paranoid wrath await those who try. We are bombarded, saturated, with the message to conform, blend, accept—be like our neighbor who is trying to be like her neighbor. We, as a culture, value the staleness of conformity over the rapture of walking in bliss. We believe the endless commercial that says (with a straight face!) that we can find ourselves, be ourselves, by buying and doing the same thing that everyone else is buying and doing.

This makes it hard for the isolated individual to be true to self. The occasional book, the rare friend, who encourages the spirit within us to come forth is like a freshet against the tide. Even though it is more painful to deny the person we've discovered we are, we endure the pain, as it's so much easier to swim with the tide. With its vast array of diversions, numbing agents, and mindbenders, the culture sees to it that it's a quiet pain.

But how do we know if we are living our Dreamway or not? By a very simple test: if we are living in the present, we are; if we are living for the future, we aren't. If life here, now, is not a Dance, then we are dead to the moment, we are giving our life away to a nebulous future. The life we are living is not ours.

The ever-present message that encourages us to live a disowned life is only heard in contemporary cultures; it does not have more than a fleeting appearance in time as life knows it. All the cultures, all the "-isms," that vie and have vied for the gift of our lives, measure their duration in terms of years, and perhaps centuries, but never in terms beyond the bounds of time and locale that would qualify any of them as intrinsic to the life-experience. There is no reason to believe that any of the present attempts at mass conformity will be any more successful at immortality. If they had beginnings, they will have ends. Is something so finite, so fleeting, worth giving our life to?

So where can we go to find ourselves? Some of us have tried the schools of higher education and have found that we must be highly attuned and extremely selective in order to ferret out the rare person of wisdom and the scant crumb of knowledge schools contain. They are the bastions of the culture, the perpetrators of the status-quo, and the trainers of those in positions of power and influence. Academic research is financed mainly by the monolithic industries and crushing armies that are so destructive of The Earth and Her People. The liberal-arts segments of universities are more nurturing and expansive, but still within culturally accepted and defined parameters.

They teach.

They teach language—mostly the language of Conquerors/Exploiters, seldom the language of an Earth People, hardly ever the language of Wolf and Wind. They teach history—mostly the history of the onrush of the great crushing civilizations, hardly ever do they guide us to the history locked in our Ancestral Memories. Those Native cultures that have survived thousands of years in prosperity, health, and Balance with The Mother are given scanty and surface coverage, while the Civilized cultures that have raised armies and built monuments and survived mere hundreds of years are studied in depth. (It is said that if we do not study and learn the lessons of history, we are doomed to repeat them. Perhaps if we study the lessons of success as ardently as the failures, we will be less apt to repeat them.) They offer coursework on the metaphysical—mostly the institutionalized philosophies of the major cultures. The world-view and spiritual wisdoms garbed in the teaching legends of the Native Peoples are presented and passed off as "myths." They teach of Earth as science—that which is quantifiable and analyzable. Seldom do they know The Great Mother to drum Her rhythm and seek Her flow. They teach power—

mostly the political, military, and economic ways of power over others, seldom the shared power of Native ways, and hardly ever the Quest for Personal Power. They teach of the workings of the mind, but little time is spent on that part of the brain that we share with our fellow animals. Hardly touched are the recesses where our instincts and intuitions lie, and where the Ancestors' voices dwell.

In this way of learning, we isolate ourselves in a box to study life outside of the box. We add another layer of isolation with the book from which we study, which is some other person's perception of that life. The third layer is the instructor, who filters the book through her perceptions. By objective definition, perceptions in and of themselves are prejudicial.

Perhaps only by intellectual construct can we overcome the inherent contradiction in attempting to know the natural realm by removing ourselves from it. However, there is little contradiction in entering an artificial environment to learn how to survive in an artificial environment.

If we do attend one of these institutions of learning, let us choose our instructors carefully, as they are more important than the area of study or course material. Some instructors have the gift of being able to spark expansiveness and inquisitiveness in their students. Many others are teaching because they are not adept at functioning in their chosen fields. Many began teaching immediately upon finishing school themselves and have no practical experience in their fields. Knowledge may come from study; wisdom comes only with age and time.

A number of prominent inventors, intellectuals, philosophers, and poets of our time have been dubbed as learning impaired, or actually mentally deficient, because they had trouble functioning within the educational system. How many potential innovators, visionaries, and individuals have been—and are being—squelched by an academic career of imposed conformity and stifled creativity?

The shame of the dominant culture is that it's possible to go successfully through life without ever developing physical form, manual dexterity, sensual acuity, innate talents, or, for that matter, spiritual attunement. Upon what strength does a culture draw when it does not inspire its people to seek their Vision, their source of Power, when it does not encourage them to develop to the fullest their physical, sensual, and creative abilities?

Cultural expectations fall into the genre of joining the religion of our parents, living in a house better than our parents, and having a higher paying job than our parents. All we have to do is show up; the rest is figured out for us—how to think, talk, act, consume, recreate. We provide the form—they shape it. It's a quiet death—a slow, sedated, mindless one. No one knows who we could have been—the songs our hearts could have brought forth, the gifts we could have bestowed upon our People.

Our nakedness has never tasted the biting sting in the smallest days of the White Season; we have never pinked to the resin-laced vapor's caress in the Sweat Lodge. Our Grandfathers have never told us stories of our Grandfather's Fathers as far back as Memories go. We have not grown up with clean Waters lapping our feet, with the dances and songs of our non-Human relations to entertain us, with the Voices in the Wind to speak to us. We were not led to seek the Vision that would give us our Song of Being. We were not nurtured on the fruit born of The Great Mother.

We do not know ourselves, because we have not been properly introduced. We do not know our Mother, because we have not been properly nourished. We do not know our Path, because our infant feet have not been placed upon it.

Immersed in this culture, where do we find the inspiration and encouragement to continue our Journey? We can seek out those whose lives are a Dance, and there are many. They just don't get much press, seldom commercial hype. Native Peoples who still walk the Old Way are living the Gift of Self and sharing that Gift with others. There are people like you and me who have discovered themselves and are returning to the Old Ways, who understand our Journey and can be of great help and encouragement. We can also look to our kin of the non-Human tribes in the natural realm. They are themselves because that is all they know; they live in the moment because that's all there is.

How do we go about seeking a Guide for our Journey? An Elder might likely answer "Go and ask the birds and rocks. Go and learn from our wild brothers and sisters who still walk the Path in Balance."

But I know you have had a childhood similar to mine; you have not been tutored in the language of the birds, you do not know your brothers to talk with them and hear their stories, you do not know your Ancestral self, the Ancients within you. So I would suggest that first you seek the Raven, and ask her to travel with you.

The Way of the Raven

One frosty spring day I went over to a friend's house to borrow a tractor. It was sitting in a clearing back in the Woods where he was using it several months back to power his small sawmill. We tried for an hour and a half to start it, finally deciding to give it one last try and then quit. Just then, Raven flew low over the clearing from the East. As I looked up, she tipped her wing toward me as a sign and disappeared over the Westward Pines. The tractor started.

Coyote, Snake, Raven, Spider—brothers and sisters who have come to us to show the way to knowledge in the natural realm. They are known for their adaptability and cunning and powers of perception. Each Native People is honored by an animal whose Path it is to share their ways of learning to Walk in Balance. Here in the Northern Forest, it is *Kagagi*—Algonquian for Raven.

Civilized People consider Raven and Crow to be the most intelligent of birds. Actually all animals are intelligent for their own kind, in the way that they need to be intelligent. It is not respectful of our kin to compare their intelligences, nor is it sensible. How can the intelligence behind the eye of Eagle be compared with the intelligence of diving Loon? In our preoccupation with our own rational-linear intelligence, we deny and belittle so much of the complex intelligences of which we are made, so it would be surprising if we did not do likewise with our other kin. (Perhaps we anthropomorphize so because we consider the apex of planetary intelligence to lie in our frontal lobes.)

Misconceptions notwithstanding, Civilized People are right in sensing something unique in Raven. To watch her mating dance in the cold, clear February sky, to watch her and Wolf play their high-risk tag game on the snow (she will land just out of his reach and taunt him—and *usually* get away), to watch her lead Wolves on the Hunt, and in thanks be given a share of the kill, to observe her performing as sentry for her other forest kin—these things speak of something extraordinary about Raven's Personal Power.

Raven is ever alert, inquisitive, guarding. Knowing her life is dependent upon the Circle beyond herself, she becomes the watchtower eyes and messenger of that Circle. To keep herself sharp and humble, she flaunts her life to her brother Wolf. Habit would be her downfall; she continually responds in unique ways to her ever-changing Circle. These are some of the gifts Raven has for us.

But she doesn't give us these gifts; as she does with Wolf, she indicates the direction of our quest; then it's up to us. She does this knowing that what we gain is not as important as how we gain it. In this way, on our quest for knowledge, we gain wisdom as we walk the path of discovery.

Wisdom has life, breath, spirit, and purpose of its own; it
holds no respect or preference for its conveyance. Nobody can
own wisdom, or keep it from another. It is independent of its
source and vehicle. It is timeless and ageless. Wisdom comes
to each of us in the way in which it is available and assimilable.
No one way is more or less right or sacred than the other. For
instance, a book may impart wisdom because there is no Elder
to do so. It is the same wisdom, just as valued and empowered.

Elderwisdom

Wisdom without the knowledge to apply it would be useless, and
knowledge without the wisdom to guide it would be a dangerous thing.
Wisdom is the fruit of knowledge sought, not knowledge memorized. In
exploring knowledge with our own senses and running it through our
own intellectual, emotional, and experiential filters, we personalize it.
This process brings us the wisdom gained in the search, which is denied
us by merely absorbing the knowledge presented by others. They still
have the accompanying wisdom, without which knowledge is like the
sweet Flower with no Breeze to carry her scent.

In the Way of Raven, the Way of self-discovery, committing to memory
is the *result* of the investigative/discovery process, rather than an end in
itself. Memory alone as a way of learning gives us more facts, but they are
less personalized. The memorizing process alone is strong on left brain,
rational-linear process, which short-circuits the Balance inherent to our
Heart-of-Hearts (that seat of wizened perspective where our senses, brain,
emotions, intuitions, the Memories, and the Life-Spirit all meet).

The guiding hand of Raven is sometimes subtle and discreet. We're not
always aware of it at first, but at some point in the future when time and
circumstance are right, the awareness will come to us, the lesson will then
be apparent. Then we'll reflect back to say, "Aah, NOW I get it; THAT'S
what she was trying to show me!"

She (or Magpie, or Otter . . .) becomes our constant companion on our
Journey. She is with each of us now, but we may not yet know her
language. We hear it, for sure, mostly as unrecognizable static. We will
likely need a Guide to attune us—a Guide who walks with Raven.

Only once did Raven visibly let her presence be known when I was in
the company of others (in the episode I related a few pages back). More
surprising was that she did it in such an overt and atypical way—she gave
me a gift! In her intercession she stepped out of character by imploring the
Powers of the Directions and her Suntrail. We'll learn of these things
further on in our Journey.

The Guide

"All that is known and all that is to be known is contained in the Book whose pages unfold as we Walk. All the words that are written and will be written, all the skills, all the knowledge of craft and herb, all the awarenesses, all the wisdom of Elders past and to come, all that ever was or will be known is ever about us in the realm of Creation. The Air, Soil, Fire, and Water, and all the beings of the rock and plant and animal clans who are made up of these, continuously pour forth this boundless wisdom."

—*She Who Talks With Loons*

There are no Teachers. We already know, or have access to, all that they know. Those who claim to be Teachers, who claim to be privy to some body of knowledge, actually do us harm, because they feed us this knowledge as it is filtered by their eyes and limited by their words. We can go to the Source ourselves and receive this knowledge directly, as it is meant for us.

When I was young, I traveled the continent in search of Teachers. I found Teachers—good Teachers, and I'm thankful for what they gave me. I was also led to several Elders who wouldn't teach me anything. I was full of questions and I was impatient to learn. But that didn't seem to matter to them; they lived in a time-frame of their own. They were patient and respectful with me (which was often more than I was with them).

What I asked for they didn't give me. They each told me it wasn't theirs to give; it was mine to find. What they did give me is perhaps the greatest gift anyone has bestowed upon me—they guided me through and beyond them to their Source of Wisdom. They did this by sharing with me the ways and language of Raven.

I came to them with an unvoiced expectation—that those who would guide me would spend a lot of time with me in helping me to seek that which I was after. One wizened Elder sensed this and addressed it with this story:

A boy of the Caribou People (the Inland Inuit) wished to become a hunter. He had an Uncle—the eldest Hunter of his relation—who had Caribou Medicine and was gifted many, many Caribou by Caribou Spirit. He provided consistently for his family, and in time of scarcity he also helped feed and clothe the less blessed.

The boy laid his Petition before the Hunter, humbly asking the Hunter to consider accepting him as an Apprentice. He spoke of his Dream, which was guiding him to bring the medicine-herbs that Caribou eat to his People so that they could be strong and warm and fleet like Caribou. He went on to say that he knew the Power of the herbs was in their flesh, and that he would have to raise his Song to Caribou Spirit on the Hunt in order to Walk his Dream.

Uncle listened with a quiet pride in his Nephew and looked off over the low-rolling Taiga as he recalled his own Petition to a great, wise Hunter of his youth. Then he spoke. The voice was his, but, in the words, the Nephew heard what was told by the great Hunter, and what was told him and his predecessors all the way back to First Hunter.

These were Uncle's words: "This old man before you is called a skilled and cunning Hunter by some. But it is Caribou Spirit who deserves the Honor, for it is she who lays the flesh of one of her own before me. And it is Wolf who has the skill and cunning; I am merely a clever imitator. You have brought your Petition to me, because you see me hunt, and you could not see who actually is the Hunter within me. I will Fast on your Petition, and if it is intended, I will accept it with Honor on behalf of the People. Then I will guide you to Wolf—the First Hunter, from whom you will learn the Hunt. This is as was done for me, and for all those of our line who have come before us."

The Teachers walk in my past, but those deep-eyed Elders still sit with me as Guides whenever Raven flaunts to tease me into an awareness or calls in warning as she circles the skies of my inner realm.

Let's not be fooled by imitations; the Guide we seek is easy to identify:

— He lives his personal Vision, and he lives in Balance. Look not to his words, or to the words of others concerning him, but read the example of self he projects—the peace about him, his physical condition, diet, shelter and lifestyle, and his involvements. Teachers often have little time to live their words and practice their craft. If they are not walking as they talk, what have they to guide others in their walking?

— He claims no special license or title, seeing himself as a fellow Seeker— as one beggar helping another to find bread.

— Most have little or no formal education, or if they do, they have been reborn after a long return to the Womb of The Great Mother.

— He is the voice of Raven; how (and if) he answers questions will show that. If he has the answers for us, he is a Teacher; if, like Raven, he answers our questions with guiding questions, and equips us with the tools to find the answers, he is a Guide.

— As the Raven responds uniquely to each changing situation, so does a Guide respond to each Seeker as a unique individual on a deeply personal Journey begging its own specific guidance. Classes, seminars, and the like are the realm of the Teacher.

— Honor and Respect are foremost in his dealings with self and others. Every act is a sacred act, as it is a step on his sacred Path and a reflection of the spirit within him.

— As Raven recognizes and plays out her role in the Greater Circle of her existence, so does a Guide use his skills and Power for the benefit of others. Giving is receiving; he is bound by Honor to guide others on their Journey as he was/is guided on his. He will not refuse an honorable request from a sincere Seeker if it is within the realm of his ability to assist.

When I seek a Guide, it is from amongst the Traditional Native or Earth Peoples of the area in which I dwell. I illustrate my rationale in the following scenario:

Imagine emigrating to a strange land with an unfamiliar climate; our clothing is unsuitable, we don't recognize the herbs and trees, we don't know the planting cycle, the patterns of the seasons, and so on. We have two choices—we can either fend for ourselves, which may take years or generations of hardship before we learn to grow into the Circle of our new existence, or we could go to the Native People and apprentice ourselves to them, accepting the benefit of their many generations of accumulated lore and wisdoms from living in Balance with the region.

We, here and now, are strangers in a strange land, not much better off than if we had just landed on the shores of the land in the above scenario. Some of us, out of fear born of the cultural and religious rigidity of our youths, and because of our disdain of self-appointed leaders and gurus, shun the voice of the Native Peoples of our new land. Instead, we may pursue an eclectic Path, picking up what feels right from this source and that, or we may choose to Walk a Path borrowed from another People in another place.

The Native People of a land know her spirits and moods, they know her herbs and medicines, they know when the berries ripen and when the fish spawn. They can sense the coming rains; in their language is the sound of the Wind and the spring birds. They are *of* the Land, as much a part of it as the Rocks and Rivers. Let us go to them to seek our Guide for our Journey back to ourselves and Our Mother.

Giving is Receiving

What is the cost of this Journey? What are we being asked to give, to let go of? Each of us must answer that for ourselves, as our Journeys are very different from one another's, and we need answers that speak our own truth. However, in support and encouragement, I can say: What cost, what shedding, is too great to hear the words our Ancestors have passed down to us, to dance with the Deer in the meadow as brothers, to find the me that vibrates with the Rhythm of the Spheres, to sing of Beauty as we thought only could the Wind and the birds, to kiss the Earth as an orphan who found her Mother?

The actual cost is something we could not imagine now and may not believe if someone tried to tell us. The cost is part of the Journey, a step in bringing its unfolding lessons before us. Any cost, any exchange for what we receive, is probably the easiest thing we will be asked to give.

A true Guide does not ask for recompense, as he knows that in giving is receiving. A true Seeker offers recompense, as she knows that in giving is receiving. It is honorable to give for what we receive, as it gives recognition to what our Guide is giving us of himself that would otherwise go to other pursuits. He may be responsible for support of self and family and he may be taking time from craft or occupation. As we give energy in exchange for that which we receive, we maintain Balance within ourselves and empower the Circle about us.

The Seeker

In the same way there are no Teachers, there are no Students. Seeker and Guide Walk the same Path, pursue the same Journey. In relation to that Journey, they are both Seekers. The only difference between them is relative; one is the elder of the other, has been Walking longer, so is more familiar with the ways of the Path.

In relation to each other, they may be sometimes Seeker, sometimes Guide. We are not at any particular place on the Path; each of us is at different places at the same time. We progress in the various aspects of our Journey at various rates. So the Seeker may well at times be as a Guide to her Guide.

The Seekers I know (myself included) are healthily schizophrenic. It is a matter of survival, as we are living an outer reality that often runs contrary to our blooming deeper self. So we cultivate a schizophrenic personality—a dual concept of reality and self, in order to sanely and honorably follow our Journey.

The Guide helps to externalize the Seeker's frustrations and contradictions so they can be recognized and dealt with. In the process the Seeker may see her Guide as the frustration or contradiction before she can recognize them as aspects of herself. He facilitates this process without her awareness so that she can approach what surfaces in her own time, by her own means and Power.

This step invariably creates a rift between Seeker and Guide—a necessary (though temporary) rift that usually perplexes the Seeker and is placidly accepted by her Guide as part and parcel to his calling.

At times the Seeker may feel hurt or grow disillusioned because she becomes aware that there are shortcuts—easier ways to learn a skill or a more direct route—that haven't been shared with her by her guide. Because he recognizes the need for her to take the step in order to understand the process and learn its lessons, he chooses not to give her the direct route. Not having his perspective, she may become angry with him when she finds out she is not being fully informed. In time she will welcome the challenges and thank her Guide as she revels in the Blessings of discovery.

The Seeker is welcomed by the Guide, because her eyes see differently than his, and her hand reaches for things his wouldn't. As he Walks with her, he is retracking himself, returning to the stretch of Path he Walked when he was as her. Through her, the Walking is this time different, unique, giving him heretofore unavailable knowledge and adding dimension to his wisdom. With this Gift, the Seeker gives great Honor to her Guide, who, in turn, holds it as a most cherished Blessing. He welcomes this Gift each time it is intended for him, because each time his Path broadens. He becomes less himself and more the Circle.

The process of seeking a Guide is the initiation to our Journey. It is a sorting process; the various Paths of Seekers and Guides merge and diverge like the interlaced Rivulets of a delta. Those of similar heart will find each other and flow together. This coming together will be different for each of us; for some it will be the result of a deliberate search, and for others, as with me, it will happen as though it was predetermined. In the latter case, one feels as though he is being expected—that the script is written, the stage is set, and he is being awaited for the drama to begin.

If the person we seek to be our Guide is of a tradition other than ours, we give him Honor and give Respect to his culture by learning the customary way of approaching and petitioning (asking) him.

Occasionally, a Seeker will find that an animal or a stone or a cloud is to be her Guide. This is a great Honor, as most of the non-Human Peoples still walk the Old Way. They are fully alive, fully attuned, and possess great wisdom. Could there be anyone better equipped to walk beside us, to emulate?

One's Guide never leaves. The Seeker grows with her Guide, and he grows into her. He becomes part of her consciousness, directing her sight and guiding her hands. He speaks to her in the Voices and guides her in Dreamtime. Like Raven, he becomes her constant companion.

An Empty Cup

A Guide asks that we approach him as an empty cup, for a full one has no room. When I first began my Journey, I was full of questions and expectations, which didn't leave room for what the Elders had to share with me, or the way they had to share it. (Now that I look back on that time, I realize how presumptuous I was to think that I could even have questions relevant to the vast, unknown Journey toward which I was making my first teetering step.) We bring to our Guide our habits, which block our ability to perceive and discover, and our surface personality, which masks our essential self, and the filters of self-pride and vanity, which fade and distort what is given to us. Approaching a Guide as an empty cup necessitates conscious work on these inhibitors to awareness and attunement.

Most of us are initially not ready or willing to do this necessary work because it is too threatening to our old self. The fear and insecurity brought on by initially facing the Journey to our intrinsic self causes our old self to react to the Path as being restricting and conforming—a path of privation and servitude. The old self may become rigid and defensive; her survival is at stake.

Giving is receiving; in order to be blessed and enriched, we may need to do some sweeping and discarding to make room, to be sure that that which we invite does not trip upon entering. And we want to be sure that our new guest finds good food and a warm bedroll to entice her to stay.

I liken our Journey to self to that of sand through an hourglass: the top orb is one of relative expansiveness and comfort, but we know there is a world beyond, for which we thirst. However, the only way to that world is through a narrow neck. In order to fit through that neck, we must trim ourselves of some of the mores and conventions that were necessary to our life in the upper orb. We will see it not as privation, but as packing lightly for the Journey and donning appropriate garb. We have caught glimpses of the new world through the narrow tunnel, so we greet our Journey as one of fulfillment rather than as a period of sacrifice. Now we can slip freely through the narrows, arriving as an empty cup.

The key to an empty cup is knowing fear, then stepping beside it. Fear is nothing more than unknowingness—apprehension of the unknown. It can catch us in a self-feeding cycle, from which it is hard to escape: Our lack of knowledge causes us to be apprehensive, which keeps us from seeking knowledge, which keeps us apprehensive . . .

We begin to step beside fear by approaching it from our place of inner Balance—what those of other persuasions would call a state of grace or higher self. When we are In Balance, we feel a connectedness with something beyond ourselves. Then we don't have to rely just upon our own knowledge and perception; our awareness of our Balance in relation to the Greater Circle allows us to feel secure in losing our old selves to that Circle, knowing that in doing so we will find our intrinsic selves. Even though we can't see much of our new world through the narrow neck we must squeeze through, we have a sense of it. Our place of inner Balance is a dimension of that world—that deeper self that is already a part of us.

Once we have stepped beside fear, the cleaning and discarding is easy. With nothing more than conscious intent, we can now approach our Guide with the humility and openness that typifies an empty cup. We can give respect to that which we do not yet know or feel, we can give thanks for that which begins to fill our cup, and we can give honor to those who guide our cup to that which flows into it.

If we are prone to biases and judgementalism, or to speaking ill of people not present, we will feel these urges subside, as they are based on fears. Rooted in lack of self-knowledge and self-concept, these fears are deep-seated.

This behavioral cycle that springs from fear often becomes a habitual defense mechanism and a means of displacing personal imbalances. It leaves slowly and painfully, because its absence exposes us and leaves us feeling vulnerable (more in the Healing chapter of Book III).

But go these displacement behaviors must, as they diffuse the Journey-Path and render the traveler impotent to a clear vision of self. They do so by externalizing and giving away our inner turmoil for others to wrestle with. This leaves us anemic and eventually bitter and self-hating, because we know ourselves only in comparison with others. Giving is receiving; when we dump our imbalances on others, they may gain by fighting our battle, but we will lose to cowardice. When we claim these behaviors as ours and do battle with them, we gain self-Honor, and the self-awareness and Personal Power that come with the victory.

I have seen some people empty their cups in the first blink of awareness as to what was holding them back, and I have seen others, gripped in fear, struggle with that awareness for many turns of the seasons. To a Guide, the time taken doesn't matter; he travels differently with time than most of us do. As soon as awareness is reached, he knows it's only a matter of time—our time—before the cup spills.

Our empty cup is ours. We fill it as we wish, and we drink as we are ready. Our Guide expects nothing of us other than what we ask of ourselves. He knows that we can receive only that which we are prepared for and open to receive. The Journey is ours; we are not taking it to please our Guide.

For some of us, beginning the Journey with an empty cup is not such a conscious process. We have reached what I refer to as a place of quiet desperation. Old patterns and habits have run their course and have bared us to the bitterness of imposed isolation from our true selves and our True Mother. We have little to risk in stepping beside our fears, little to gain in defending our old self. We are already at the threshold with our tipped-over cup, already open, already thirsting. Our Guide has an easy time introducing us to Raven and the Ways of the Path, because we've sunk so low that we've kissed the Earth, and now we're ready to Walk in that kiss.

The Only Step

We are now ready to begin the Journey. Most journeys are a series of steps, but this one is only one step—the one we are presently taking. Sometimes a step takes half a lifespan, sometimes it is so short it rattles within the time of a heartbeat. There is no knowing when the step is completed but from the perspective of the next step.

Total immersion and expansion into the present step is being *alive*. Some of us continue growing into our steps until our last breath, while some of us, trying to get into the next step prematurely, succeed, thereby adulterating the present step. No longer living in the moment's step, we rediscover time and become walking dead.

One pitfall that can get us skipping is the class or workshop that advertises to progress us a step along on our Path. If that workshop is our next step and if it junctures with our Path in a timely fashion, we can only gain by participating. If it is not in rhythm with our Path, it can get us skipping over steps and missing their lessons, thereby losing ourselves to our unfolding. These missed lessons would have given us the capacity and background to recognize, comprehend, and assimilate the knowledge and wisdoms of coming steps.

The paradox is that we are not sufficiently wizened or attuned to perceive the next step until we have completed the present one. Berries cannot be gathered until the completion of their growing and ripening season. Our Journey is akin to our first berrying season; we don't know what to expect or when. If we try to skip over one of the growing or ripening steps, we would have no harvest.

Our Guide has walked many Journeys; he has an intrinsic feel for their rhythm and season. When such paradox arises, he will help keep us directed in the Way that brings the fullness of self-discovery to our Journey.

Honor for Another's Path

Birds migrate with only their kind even though all birds are going in the same direction, at the same time, and to the same place. So too do we each Walk our Journey. Perhaps our Path winds through different terrain than the next person's, and perhaps that person's Guide speaks in ways that do not touch us. Sometimes people utter words of intolerance and condemnation of another's Path because they don't understand it. Let us remember that each of us is on a Journey that is very personal and unique; it is not intended that we understand the Journey of another. We do not know that person's language; we have not walked in that person's steps. When we step back and see through the eyes of the Circle beyond ourselves, we find that all the diverse rivulets eventually make their way to the same Ocean, and that all the birds, as different as they are in color, shape, and size, make their Journey equally well.

Elders
Dr. Seuss, *Green Eggs and Ham*
The Elves and the Shoemaker—a fairy tale (Also known as *The Secret Shoemaker*)

II

The Old Way Culture

Is there still life in the Rocks, does Father Sun still visit the dawn, does the She Swallow diving at our heads in defense of her young on the limb above still Walk the Path?

Introduction to Part II

In a despondent mood on a warm, grey afternoon, I asked Talks With Loons if the Old Way is forever gone from this land, if the few aged Healers and Grandmothers are the last vestiges of a way of life in its death-throes. I didn't know whether she'd answer directly, as her way was more often that of subtle Raven. For a few long minutes she became absorbed in reflection, during which she directed me with her eyes to observe the prairie about us. Then her gaze lost its focus as it seemed to flow into and dwell within the panorama before us, and she spoke:

"Is there still life in the Rocks, does Father Sun still visit the dawn, does the She-Swallow diving at our heads in defense of her young on the limb above still Walk the Path? The Old Way was not born with our species and it will not be buried with our species. As we sit here, the Grasses in the fullness of their bloom whisper teachings that were secret to us yesterday. As long as the Grass shall grow, as long as the Rocks are here to speak, the Old Way survives."

I was once taught that the Old Way culture was the language, crafts, and rituals of a People; I have since been shown that these are but its most surface, visible expression—the social medium in which a People is immersed. The Old Way is the Ancestral Memory—that cumulative primal knowledge rooted in my reptilian brain, which is expressed in my instincts and intuitions. It is the way my physical self has evolved to function in its rhythm, the way my senses are pre-tuned to its language. It is the only way I know, as I was born into it eons before I took my first breath. It is the way a Fox walks through the grass, the way a Flower drinks water, the way a Rainbow is. It is the way of all Creation, the way of all through whom flows The Breath of Life.

When I leave the ungiving pavement and the soft duff
of the Forest again pads my feet, I know I'm back home.

Who Are We?

Perhaps the most powerful evidence we have as to who we are is the deep, rejuvenating feeling that is engendered when we spend some time close to The Earth. When I leave the ungiving pavement and the soft duff of the Forest again pads my feet, I know I'm back home. Like a lost puppy returned, I spontaneously relax into Her comfort and trust in Her nourishment.

We are Clan Earth Peoples, or perhaps I should say, we are *still* Clan Earth Peoples. Our natural home is still as close to the Earth and Sky as we can be. Those of us who have dwelled for generations in the cities are still drawn to The Earth when we can get away on vacations.

Our eyes are healthier and less stressed in the green light that filters through a canopy of trees. We have the innate capacity to trust and share with only a maximum of fifteen to twenty-five people. We haven't existed enough generations to genetically change and adapt to our altered world, to which the "diseases of civilization" are testament.

Stress-related diseases are the classic voice screaming at us of our intolerance of the Civilized Way. It is classic because our success in the dominant culture is directly proportional to our tolerance of stress. Production, organization, regimentation, and specialization on the level needed to sustain the Civilized Way create a continual high-stress climate. This causes conflicts and contradictions within us, as we're not equipped to deal with such stress. We evolved in a living situation where stress was periodic and short-lived. In activities such as the Hunt, stress played a part in stimulating adrenal function, and sharpening alertness and sensual perception. There was a gradual buildup, a climax, and a quick release. We, as a species, haven't evolved the capacity to handle continual stress normally. So we do what we can to ease the pain and placate the inner warriors—drugs, alcohol, meditation, counseling, stress management workshops, and so on. Sometimes we lose control of the inner battle and it externalizes in the form of mental, digestive, and cardiovascular disease, addictions, domestic violence, and suicide.

We find other evidences and surviving remnants of who we (still) are disguised and buried in some of the least likely of places. For example, the following "Hagar the Horrible" comic strip illustrates the Old Way concept of staying clear to the moment by bringing resolution as close as possible to the time of conflict:

We find other evidences and surviving remnants of who we (still) are,
disguised and buried in some of the least likely of places.

It is hard to seek our identity through the study of self because it is difficult to step back and observe. Our kin of the natural realm have identities intrinsic to them, no matter what their cultural surroundings; we Humans have a much more malleable consciousness, which can cloud our essential beings. But we can see our innate reflection in those who Walk the Old Way, as they have an identity that is intrinsic to their life experience. And we can see ourselves in our natural environment because we are the product and sum total of that environment, and we are nothing out of its context. Our non-Human kin in that realm are as we would be in an unadorned, unfettered (i.e., uncivilized) state.

. . . in Relation to Native People?

When I began my own search for who I was in relation to The Mother, I thought it was presumptuous of me to imagine that I could be an Earth Person. I felt self-conscious and out of place when I sought out the Native Elders and Teachers I was being drawn to. I had no lineal or cultural connection—nothing to ground me. Or so I thought.

Then Raven, in her subtle way, drew the essence out of my cluttered searchings and gave it back to me. That clarity freed me of the stereotypes as to who I was and who I wasn't. I was able to begin hearing the voices of those around me who knew me, knew my Ancestors.

What they told me was hard to fathom—that my Ancestors, the Native People of Europe, Walked the Old Way just as did the Native People of America. In the same ways they hunted and foraged, sought Vision, entered the Sweat Lodge, and lived in Clan-Circles around the Drum and Moon. One not specializing in their study would be hard-pressed to distinguish their wigwams, arrowheads, and clothing one from the other. The lifeways of both were crushed by the Civilized Conquerers; both were forced/coerced to take new ways and shun their own as being of the Devil.

The Drums of both were destroyed, shearing their connectedness with the Earth and each other, robbing their collective source of Power. The voices went on to say that the only significant difference between me and my regional Native neighbors is the number of generations we are removed from our Earth/Clan roots.

Their recent forebears who lived the Old Way have more in common with my Old Way forebears than with their Aztec and Inca kin (whose ways of slavery, class, taxation, war, wealth amassment, and Human sacrifice gave them a closer cultural and spiritual relationship to some of my Civilized European kin than to my Native neighbors).

Even more profound to me was their sharing that the Blood and Ancestral Memories of my forebears live on in the American Natives—that we are cousins. They showed me the writings in the old script of my People scattered across this land; they showed me the stone ceremonial structures and observatories that my People built; they showed me remnants of my ancestral language that still exist in Native tongues spoken here, today. They told me of the legends that recount the day when my People were here and also foretold of their return. They showed me accounts of the Post-Columbian explorers that speak of the light-haired, blue-eyed People they encountered amongst the Natives. And they drew me into the legends and ceremonies that still carry the clear imprint of my People from the time when they first walked this land.

They came—Celts, Norse, Carthaginians, Hebrews, Libyans. They may have already been coming 5,000 years ago, to trade and mine and fish. Some of them stayed, intermarried, and helped to found many of the present tribes. For example, Zuni language and pottery styles are based on ancient Libyan; the Pima, whose language is Semitic in origin, still sing a literal version of the creation legend of their Semitic Phoenician Ancestors; the Algonquian languages are laced with Egyptian, Norse, and Celtic words.

Elders of the Old Way tell me that we are all the same—we all have red blood and white bones, we are all children born of the same Mother. That being so, they say that the Way of Our Mother—the Old Way—has to be intrinsic to all. Conditioning is what makes some of us Civilized. It channels our natural spiritual inclinations into some Religion and diverts our foraging instincts into some grocery store.

Some People of all the races have been Civilized for millenia (including the Red Race, whose empires we recently mentioned). And there are still some of each race who live the Old Way, such as the Ainu and Sami (Laplanders) of the White Race.

This being the case, perhaps those who distinguish Conquerer and Conquered, Civilized and Native, by race are not using a valid criteria. In fact, the concept of race appears not to hold up well to observation. If we were to travel westward from Southeast Asia, we would notice the Mongoloid features of the People we pass gradually softening as Caucasoid characteristics grew stronger. We'd find a comparable transition on a trek through Europe to Africa. As we went southward we would observe the People getting progressively darker. Caucasoid features would continue to fade as Negroid features strengthened and finally reached the fullness of their expression in Central Africa. A trip across pre-Columbian America would reveal similar, varying blends of Mongoloid, Caucasoid, and Polynesian characteristics.

So where do we draw the lines to categorize ourselves by race? Perhaps we are more like a Rainbow, which owes its beauty—and its very existence—to its various hues blending and unfolding into one another.

Elders
Barry Fell, *America, B.C., Bronze Age America, Saga America*
Salvatore Trento, *The Search for Lost America*
Jennings Wise, *The Red Man in the New World Drama*

The food had a life and a spirit that was given to it by their hands . . .

The Old Way and Civilization

The Old Way is the way of living common to the Native Peoples of The Earth, no matter what the era, culture or region. It is also the way of the plants, the animals, the Air, and the Water. It is the way all things natural were, are, and will be. This timeless Way is called "old" only by those who have abandoned it and now measure time in passing. Few Humans in this day know it or live it.

Civilization is the lifeway of Peoples who control and regiment the natural order. It is the current lifeway of most Humans, and of the animals, plants, and environments they have harnessed or domesticated to live it.

In these next few pages we will explore both Ways in order to gain a perspective on the crest we Walk between the Path behind and the Path ahead. Then we will leave Civilization for the rest of our Walking together. (This chapter is an oversimplification of the two Ways and in some cases a comparison of incomparables. I am taking license for effect—to bring us quickly to the Spirit and Fire of our Journey.)

A Comparison

I recently met an Elder who gave me a most beautiful description of the Old Way in two words—*sharing* and *kindness*. Exploring the folds and reflections of those two words gives a full and lush view of that lifeway. The same day another Elder was speaking of the concerns she had for her grandchildren being exposed to the dominant culture. In elaborating on her fears, she gave a succinct, three-word definition of Civilization—*individualism*, (the accumulation of) *possessions*, and *commercialism*.

This dichotomy leaves little wonder that the Conquerors' first reaction to Native Peoples is often one of revulsion and sub-human classification. The Conquerors see them as crazy savages, fighting against all odds in a war they cannot win. The most spiritual often appear to be the most warlike. The intruders cannot grasp that the People are defending what they see as their clear right to follow Spirit. They are fighting for the very life and health of their Mother. They see it as better to die in Her defense than for them, and their generations to follow, to live a life of subjugation and encagement. Such a life would mean being forced not only to witness, but to be an active part in, the slow poisoning and dismemberment of the Sacred Mother-Source. In the end the People can find pride in losing, while the Civilized hordes can only find shame in winning.

Civilized People are still conquering Native People, though with the complexity of the contemporary world political-economic structure, perhaps not as conspicuously as in past centuries. With the consumption of every fast-food burger goes a chunk of South American Rainforest four times the area of my Lodge. (The Rainforest is one of the last holdouts of the People.) The purchase of every Japanese product pushes the Ainu—the indigenous (and Caucasian) Old Way Japanese People—closer to the sea on the last, northernmost island they inhabit.

Conquerors are prone to defining their morality quite narrowly, which helps justify their ways. For instance, they found it hard to reconcile the fact that the Hopi, whom they viewed as a peaceful, agricultural, and very spiritual People, commonly had extramarital relations; while the Apache, whom they regarded as heartless plunderers, were morally conservative and very strict concerning mated fidelity. Even something as seemingly innocuous as dance was intolerable to the Conquerors; they could not accept it as being more than just social entertainment. (Native Peoples, for whom dance is a central spiritual, psychological, and cultural expression, were equally surprised when they found out that Civilized dance was *just* social.)

Some primary distinctions between Civilized People and Native People: The Civilized change the world to suit themselves, while the Native adapt themselves to the world as it is; the Civilized are ever discontent with their present situation and dedicate their entire lives to changing it, while the Native are ever thankful for the beauty and bounty they find themselves immersed in; the Civilized dwell in the errors of the past and the hope of the future, while the Native bask in the fullness of the moment; the Civilized draw everything toward themselves while the Native become *of* everything about them; the Civilized grovel and beg as they contritely pray, while the Native pridefully sing in praise, thanksgiving, and wonderment; the Civilized have psychologists to help them adjust to their unreasonable lives, while the Native live in the harmony of their environs; the Civilized have religion, the Native live religion; the Civilized talk a lot, the Native listen and learn. The Civilized admire each other for *what* they are; the Native admire each other for *who* they are. The Civilized meet death lying in bed expending every effort to further extend life, while the Native greet death upright, if possible, with their Song of Passing on their lips as they greet the New Cycle.

Civilization is based on Human-made things that keep breaking down; the Old Way is based on natural things, which keep growing, renewing. Human-made things need regular input, while natural things keep giving.

Civilized People become enslaved to their possessions, ever working to maintain them, while Native People are as free and unencumbered as the natural things that provide their needs.

Work as a concept is known only to Civilized People. It was born of the necessity to support the individualism and material opulence intrinsic to the lifeway. Where Natives avoid unneccesary duplication by sharing tools and other resources, Civilized People strive to individually possess whatever they use. They lead a catch-22 existence—they buy houses and cars so they can get jobs, then they have to keep their jobs so they can support their houses and cars. Their houses bulge with specialized rooms that are little used, while the lodges of Natives are small and open, designed for multiple usage of space (more in Wigwam chapter of Book III).

The material comparisons go on, but this will suffice to illustrate that Civilized People are working largely for things they don't use. They are committed to payments, taxes, insurance, maintenance, utility bills, and so on, no matter if or how much their material goods are used.

Their "labor saving" devices actually save them little; the time saved is consumed by working elsewhere to pay for the tool, its fuel, maintenance, and the costs of storage. Some appliances, such as the washing machine, are not timesavers for an additional reason—their advent enabled more consumption. Now people have more clothes, and change and wash them more often, spending just as much time on laundry as before the machine.

Native People require but an average of two hours a day to provide their needs and desires, no matter whether the environment is lush tropic or desert. Their rich cultures, strong families, and lavish handiworks attest to their bountiful spare time. Their labor applies directly to their needs, as opposed to the more abstract Civilized concept of "going to work" to provide needs in a less direct way. Simply put, Natives transfer energy efficiently by direct involvement in what they need; whereas Civilized People, through a complex and non-personally involved process, expend much more time and energy to meet the same need. For instance, when Native People desire fruit, they will simply go and pick it, whereas Civilized People will buy land, and go through the process of raising the fruit before picking it, or "go to work" to pay someone else to raise (package, store, and transport) it for them.

Those who have lived both Ways talk of the richer, more fulfilling life of the Native Way, with its direct involvement in the process of existence, as compared with the detached, indirect means of the Civilized Way. I first felt this difference when I was invited to share a meal with a Native family. The food had a life and a spirit that was given to it by their hands as they hunted, gardened, foraged, stored, prepared, and served it. This was reflected in the Blessing of the food, the way it was presented, eaten, and enjoyed, and in the way it was valued and respected, without a bite being wasted. What a blessed experience when compared to my hollow store-bought meals!

There is little sacred in Civilized societies. They are systems-oriented; they look to structure for answers, not knowing of the ways of Elders and the Talking Circle and the Inner Voice. The once-sacred becomes lowered to the Civilized society's secular norm. Drugs, alcohol, and sex become objects of pleasure, where in the few Native societies where drugs or alcohol are used, they are used sporadically, and as part of sacred rituals (see Alterants chapter in Book II).

Civilized People are ego-sensitive; self-recountings of their adventures and successes often come across as self-aggrandizing and ego-threatening to the listener. In cultures where the Warrior and the Healer and the Seeker still exist, stories of their Journeys and triumphs are regularly told and eagerly awaited. Beyond entertainment, these recountings serve as teachers and examples to inspire and emulate. Perhaps because Native People have more opportunity for self-fulfillment than their Civilized counterparts, they are less threatened and more inspired by the success of others.

My impression is that the unspoken Civilized objective is to fashion an Earth (and beyond?) that is under total Human control. What Native People see as their natural realm, Civilized People see as uncontrolled, wild. Their neighbors are no longer the animals and plant People, but other Humans. So the natural realm is truly wild to them, and their isolation from it isolates them from its care, and from its wisdoms. For an example, with many non-Human People, staring into another's eyes is a sign of assertiveness and dominance, or of aggression. It is also a giveaway to the stalked and a preoccupation that puts one out of contact with the Greater Circle. For these reasons, Natives consider it foolish and disrespectful to stare into the eyes of another, particularly an Elder. No longer knowing the animals to gather these lessons, Civilized People suffer interactions plagued with the friction of their eyes and the imbalance of their perception.

Civilized Peoples' care for the Source of their goods is not sensitive to Her needs because they do not know Her needs. For example, when logging for their lumber and paper, they don't know to let some of the big, hollow trees stand, so one-quarter of the varieties of our bird kin are left homeless.

One reason for the "success" of the Civilized Way is its willingness to adopt the ways of other cultures that work to its advantage. This approach has created functional cultures but without the Ancestral roots and spiritual bases of the cultures from which they borrow. For example, they have borrowed practices from the people of India, such as what they call Yoga and Transcendental Meditation. They are fragments of a Hindu People's life-approach, surface techniques which are a reflection of the underlying philosophy. Only the exercise is desired; its spirit is left behind. This allows for Civilization's penchant to commercially exploit other cultures. So we see these borrowed practices being promoted with such lines as "Reduce stress, increase productivity, lose weight, be a better yuppie or salesman by practicing . . . " The Civilized Way could benefit greatly from a deeper look at and understanding of the ways of other cultures, but instead it is content skimming the grease off the top and using it to lubricate the worn-out mechanism of its lifeway.

The Civilized Way can be characterized by such contemporary cliche's as, "the me generation," "self-development," and "I do my thing, you do yours." The most powerful contemporary response that I've heard is Albert Schweitzer's, which echoes Old Way wisdom, "Life outside a person is an extension of the life within him. This compels him to be part of it and accept responsibility for all creatures great and small. Life becomes harder when we live for others, but it also becomes richer and happier."

Where They Diverged

If we are all the same People, where did our Paths diverge and some of us turn from The Mother to see if we could do better? Perhaps the answer lies in the way we look at a seed. Agriculture is the basis of Civilization; with it came permanent settlements and the concept of land ownership. The Earth became "property"—a despiritualized, inanimate commodity. Now Civilization had a foundation upon which to lay its cornerstones— the concentration of wealth and power, predatory trade and warfare, and the enslavement of Humans, animals, plants, Water, and minerals.

The Old Way, based on foraging economies dependent upon a respectful relationship with Earth, can give no root or nourishment to the above-mentioned Civilized traits. Nor can it support cultural, economic, and political stratification. Instead, its small interactive groups, which share in spirit, strife, and pleasure, encourage a more personally involved, less bounded lifeway.

Native village soil-tillers became the transitional step between the Old Way and Civilization. It is here that we first see powerful leaders, class systems, and wealthy individuals. It is also here where interest, rent, currency, and animal and human sacrifice make their entrance, as they are largely absent from the lifeways of foraging Peoples.

Old Way Primitive

The term *primitive* is often associated with People Walking the Old Way. Many who use the term in this context define it as *crude, unevolved, basic*; whereas it actually means nothing more than *first*. Leading a primitive life involves a high degree of mental, physical, and spiritual attunement, sensual acuity, and skills development.

To illustrate this point to the skeptic, I ask him to make Fire, and I in turn do the same. As he is digging in his pocket for a match to strike or a Bic to flick, I am preparing my bow and drill Firemaking kit to release the Sun Spirit locked in the wood. A few seconds after his match is burned out, I'm blowing life into the coal nestled in my tinder. Then I invite him to try my method, and I ask to try his. I master his technique in mere seconds whereas he has trouble grasping even the rudiments of mine. Not surprising, as it takes weeks of practice—even when coming from a place of attunement—to become proficient at the bow-and-drill method.

I can draw examples from all the aspects of spiritual and physical life to demonstrate which way of life really fits the Civilized definition of primitive, but the above usually proves adequate.

Civilized People live in linear fashion, with their lives and fortunes beginning at birth, progressing through life and ending at death. They view the life of their societies in the same way. The Circle symbolizes the way Native People perceive these things. On the next page we'll enter that realm.

Elders

Morris Berman, *Coming to Our Senses. The Reenchantment of the World.*
Forrest Carter, *The Education of Little Tree*
Robin Clarke and Geoffrey Hindley, *The Challenge of the Primitives*
Frederick Gearing, *The Face of the Fox*
Robert Holdstock, *The Emerald Forest* (Also available as a video movie.)
Theodora Kroeber, *Ishi in Two Worlds*
Ursula K. LeGuin, *The Word for the World is Forest* (Also available on voice cassette.)
Jerry Mander, *In the Absence of the Sacred*
Jack Weatherford, *Indian Givers: How the Indians of the Americas Tranformed the World*

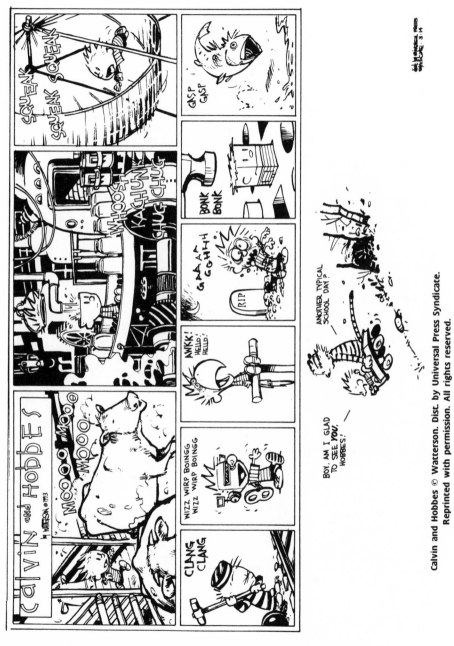

*No one knows who we could have been—the Songs our hearts could have
brought forth, the Gifts we could have bestowed upon our People.*

All of our Earth relations are part of this rhythm in which we vibrate.

The Sacred Circle

As I walk toward Woods' edge, the two Ravens I just caught in the act of stealing Duck eggs sound their minor threat/alert alarm. A Bluejay, searching the bark folds of a Birch Tree for the last of her stowed away acorns, carries the call deeper into the Forest. She sets the Red Squirrels achatter and the Nuthatches flit and "peent" a bit more nervously than usual around the tree trunks. Further in the Woods, a browsing pregnant Doe and her two lingering offspring of the previous year pick up the alarm, raise their heads and cock their ears in an effort to pick up some sign of the disturbance. I'm catching just a fragment of the leading edge of a ripple that began because I took a few steps off the trail to investigate the sheening black presence under a Blackberry tangle. As I high-step over the Blueberries to return to the trail, I begin to consider the affect of my actions. . .

The Circle in which we exist is bounded by the limit of our influence and perception—both actual and potential. This Circle is constantly vascillating with the ebb and flow of the energies within and about us. Each step, each pulse of emotion, each word we read, contorts a segment of that Circle. The Circle is two-faceted, existing both within and beyond us. In that we are the sum total of our environment and perceptual experiences, both external and internal, the bounds of the Circle are the bounds of self.

There are Circles within Circles; our visual Circle may not necessarily be our hearing Circle. The various Circles of which we are comprised are in a constant flowing state of overlap, coalescence, and divergence.

The meeting of Circles emanating from various sources forms the Web of Life. These areas of overlap create the dynamic that gives life its richness and dimension. I liken it to a quiet pool in which pebbles are being tossed: Each pebble causes concentric Circles to emanate from it, which overlap the concentric Circles of other pebbles. This vast and complex interplay of Circles upon Circles—of Circles combining and reforming themselves, reflecting off the shore and lapping themselves—is the Web of Life.

Everything affects everything (which makes our every action important—a matter of Spirit). The breath I am now taking sends a ripple that will travel to the farthest reaches of the universe and will take part in affecting all manner of occurrences. It will come back to me in many and diverse ways. Some of the purveyors of doctrine and creed tend to simplify this awareness and place us Humans at its cause-and-effect center, calling it karma, hell, justice. The Lifespirit flows beyond the bounds of rational concept, oblivious to one-dimensional views of flow, and cerebrally fueled predator-conqueror views of self-importance.

The Circle also takes concrete dimension in the natural world as the predominant form and organization of matter and energy. From den and tree to Sun and sand, the Circle is and the Circle is becoming. Upheavals—the overlapping ripples of Circles—appear as forms other than Circles (e.g. mountains, cathedrals, 'line' of sight). But closer inspection shows these angular forms to be comprised of Circles. The perspective of distance shows them to be no more than the ripples of a greater Circle. The perspective of time shows their sharp edges ever softening back toward the Mother-form of the Circle through the effect of other ripples—erosion, decay, destruction.

The Circle is nourishing to the spirit. We react more congenially to a curved shape than an angular one. My civilized realm acknowledges this with such terms as *well-rounded* (meaning well-balanced) and *square* (out of date, socially inept). Sitting in a Circle with others encourages trust and sharing; living in a circular lodge imparts a feeling of security and comfort. Moon and Sun and Earth—those sources of Life and Power that we hold sacred—imprint their shape upon everything they touch and nourish and create. Our first home is the womb, our second home is our mother's arms; our first sights are of her breast and of her face—warm, first Circles so strongly and deeply imprinted that we spend the rest of our lives trying to return to them. We find them again in our lovers' embrace, in the Circle of our family, in the Womb of the Sweat Lodge.

We live on in the moment not as a conscious being, not as an individual entity, but as the present embodiment and conveyance of that which our Ancestors have brought forth to gift to their future grandchildren. At the same time, we are a road carrying the ripples from the past and a crossroad where other ripples from the present continuously lap them. This lapping is a selective process that clashes and weakens some ripples from the past and combines with and strengthens others. We pass this new/old gift on as each moment melts into the next and we eventually become one with the Ancients in the continuum to our far-distant children's children's children.

We are Ancients at the same time we are children, because we are giving to the future as do Ancients, and we are receiving from the past as do children. In this way we have no perspective of beginning or end, birth or death. We were alive long before we were born, and we will live long after we die. At this moment we are each young and old, dying and being reborn. We are and continually experience each of these things, because our identity is not us, but that which flows through us. So there is no progression in life—only the continual flow of a stream that keeps coming upon itself, keeps giving itself waters old and waters new, waters to be and waters that were. Grandchildren come around to become parents to their Ancestors. This is the Hoop of Life.

We are a point on that Circle—a unique point of synthesis of ripples that have never before touched, and at the same time we are many points, because we are of many ages and times. Circles overlap, as many strings of Ancestors walk within us, and many strings of children walk from us. So at the same time we are a point on many Circles, which touch each other, merge, and separate in perpetual rhythm.

All of our Earth relations are part of this rhythm in which we vibrate. In the same way that our Ancestors and our children become and travel through us, so do the Birds and the Hills and the Rain. They, too, have Ancestors and children, who are continually reborn through each other in their own Circles and who become our Ancestors and children also as our Circles meet.

Any approach to the Old Way begins with this awareness of the Circular view of life, which is shared by all Native People. It permeates the fabric of their lives and reflects in their everyday activities: They enter and leave their lodges and ceremonial Circles in Sunwise fashion (clockwise, or as Sun travels the sky, as the seasons rotate). Their villages are laid out in a Circle, they sit in a Circle at council. They bring their Elders to their offspring to make their life a Circle.

> circles in a season
> circles in a song
> spring comes around
> to circle winter long
>
> spirit in frog
> spirit in tree
> all are one
> with the spirit in me

> —*from a Totem song*

*As I came of age as a Seeker, Dolphin and Mosquito . . .
began sharing with me their Traditions . . . .*

Tradition as a River

In my early adulthood I wandered this Land in search of some cultural foundation. Stories I'd been told of an old Medicine Man drew me to his High Desert camp. He was off conducting a Healing when I arrived, so his people invited me to stay until his return and graciously accommodated me.

They gave me lodging in one of their Wickiups—lodges built by the weaving together of Willow branches. The interior of the Wickiup gave me the feeling of being inside a great, inverted Willow basket. Four directional posts supported a storage platform in the center of the lodge. That night, I fell asleep to the sweet smell of Willow and the comforting feeling engendered by a warm Fire and the patina of old ways.

At first light, I was awakened by a faceless voice at my door directing that I appear momentarily at the Ceremonial Circle. Within the time it took me to dress, I blinked off as much of the weariness of travel as I could and went off into the dry, chill air to answer the summons.

All of the adults of the camp were already assembled in silence. I found a place in the Circle, and the Sun Greeting Ceremony began. The language was foreign to me and the unfamiliar movements caused me to feel like a stand-in actor who had no opportunity to rehearse.

I gave my hosts a day of labor and was back on the road before nightfall.

When I was younger, I was obsessed with things traditional and kept a berth between me and anything that wasn't. I sought traditional lore and knowledge in museums, books, and from Keepers of the Old Ways commonly referred to as Traditionals. As I came of age as a Seeker, Dolphin and Mosquito (two of my animal Guides; see Book III) began sharing with me their Traditions, leading me to the threshold of an awareness that spun me around and left me wide-eyed to this day.

I used to see things traditional as old, stable, hallowed, and unquestioned. In the search for tradition, my perspective was not much distant from that of many academics of the archaeology and cultural anthropology fields. I read their stuff and retraced their steps and I sought the Elders who shared of Tradition.

The Awareness

One day after wise Raven began to walk with me, I heard a song at a Traditional ceremony that didn't sound quite like the other songs. After the ceremony I talked about the song with two people present who I felt might be able to address the impression the song gave me. They were both taken aback by my questioning something Traditional and assured me that if the song was a part of sacred ceremony, it was preserved and passed down to us from ancient times. It would have been sacrilegious for them to question; they accepted and duplicated.

Later, I did some research on the song: The melody was borrowed from a French folksong and the words were of a common Christian prayer translated into the Old Tongue. Thus began the demystification of Tradition as it was presented to me.

Shortly thereafter, I was speaking with a Traditional Healer, who told me that for fourteen generations now the Tradition of her Native People has been Christianity. I knew this to be a historical fact, but I never thought about it in the same light as when it was told to me by a Traditional. I was told further that many of the People are not consciously aware of this source and influence on their Traditions. Soon after, I began developing a knack for discerning what is intrinsically of the People, and what was bestowed upon them by the Conquerors.

The final dash to my dogmatic approach to tradition came about when I became aware of the origins of one of the organizations of Native Healers in my area. This group is a powerful and regarded bastion of the healing craft, considered by Native and academic alike to be an ancient Medicine Way. Nevertheless, I saw in it too much of the Civilized Way not to question its roots. My own research showed that it probably did not exist before the days of the fur trade. Influenced by the pomp and hierarchical structure of the Catholic Church, the economic structure of the French traders and their accompanying spiritual and secular values, the Medicine People joined to contemporize their indigenous art.

The River

Tradition for the sake of tradition, tradition as a rigid set of archaic structures demanding unerring allegiance is not and has not been part of the Old Way. Tradition distinguishes one People from another; it is the conveyor of a People's culture, the element that gives it span and continuity over the generations. It is the voice and the hand of the Ancestors, bringing to the present the skills mastered, lessons learned, spirits voiced, ventures and merriment had, so that succeeding generations can benefit from the experiences. It is the sole element responsible for the evolution of a People, as it would be impossible for each new generation to live all the experiences and come to all the wisdoms and insights that tradition gives them.

Traditions have unique flavors and textures. Each one is well suited to the environment in which it evolved, as The Mother in the lush variance of Her countenance provides a special experiential arena for each. So misplaced traditions often run amuck, as they're out of their environmental context. And hybridizing traditions often spawns bastard offspring that are short-lived, as they have their roots to the sky.

Living traditions are ever vibrant, ever changing, in light of new experiences and the new needs of present and coming generations. Every generation adds to the body of tradition, and still it can be easily recognized as the same tradition over a span of many hundreds and even thousands of years. The oldest elements of tradition are most often retained, because, by so often and for so long being tested and retested, they continually prove and reaffirm their value and depth. Sometimes a new addition lasts long enough to become part of the hallowed body of tradition, but most often not. This newcomer is attempting to travel the generations in elite company; in order to maintain that company, it must pass the most severe and continuous test—that of time.

If we live with people, we are part of a culture, we share in a tradition. We can choose the cultural environment we immerse ourselves in, or we can accept by default the one in which we find ourselves. Culture shapes and tradition feeds the tree upon which the leaves of our lives unfold, so let's choose rather than accept.

Moon's cycle . . . affects the rhythm of all of our physical and spiritual energies.

Time and Moons

Moon as Sister

The celestial bodies touch our lives in ways that are dramatic and subtle, complex and simple. Those who walk the Civilized Way have, through isolation, become desensitized to much of this effect on their lives. Earth and Sun, by far the most dominant, are largely taken for granted.

There is renewed interest in astrology—the ancient craft of determining celestial influence on our lives. However, the subtle effects of the other planets barely rate in comparison to Moon, which profoundly affects the movement, reproductive, and growth rhythms of everything on Earth. Beyond astrology's underplaying of the influence of Sister Moon, so close and such a powerful companion on our lifewalk, She is relegated mainly to a role in poetry, romance, and Halloween.

Yet the remnants of more conscious times past echo on in the Civilized languages: *Month* is derived from Moon—reflective of when time was chronicled by the Lunar cycle; *Menses*, an old form of the word Moon, survives from the time when women still felt the Lunar pull regulating their reproductive cycles.

The names of the months hearken back to the time when each Moon-cycle was known for its gifts: *January* is derived from Janus, the Roman guardian-spirit of beginnings and endings (as this is the time when one year-cycle ends and another begins); *May* is named for Maia, the Greek goddess of fertility and growth.

Like so many numbers, the names of the months have become meaning-less labels to distinguish one time period from another. This came about partly because of the uneven number of Lunar cycles in a full turn of the seasons (about 12 1/3) which did not fit well with expanding Civilization's increasing need for structure and standardization. So the lengths of the months were arbitrarily adjusted to fit neatly into a year, thereby losing sync with Moon.

The Christian Church, wanting to disassociate the "heathen Moons" from sanctified time-telling, also played a role in establishing the non-Moon-based months just mentioned. This resulted in the Gregorian calendar, now used by most Civilized People. In doing so, the Church ceased recognizing the primordial connection of the time-cycle of our species with the time-cycle of Sister Moon. (Still, the Church fell short of a complete purge; movable feasts such as Easter are still determined by the Lunar calendar.)

But Moon lives on within us, despite the concerted denial of Her force in our lives. Our biological cycles evolved in sync with Moon's rhythms. This is no more apparent than in a woman's estrus cycle, which is referred to by Native People as her Mooncycle. (We learn more of woman's Mooncycle in the chapter entitled Sisters of the Moon.) The Moon is so closely associated with fertility that She is considered female. Because there can be no pregnancy before a woman's first Mooncycle, Native People recognize and honor the close physical and spiritual bond between woman and Moon. (Please note that a woman can become pregnant before the first visible sign that she has entered her first Mooncycle, because menses occurs at the end of the cycle.)

Moon's cycle also evidences itself in all people, as well as plants, animals, and The Earth. It affects the rhythm of all of our physical and spiritual energies. These patterns will unfold as we Walk further on in this Journey together.

Moon as Time

The calendar as we know it traces its earliest roots to the desire of sedentary agricultural Peoples to keep accurate track of the dates of harvest and planting, and the rituals attendant to them. Those involved in the trade, seafaring, and political/military activities that a stable agricultural base affords found the calendar a benefit as well. They needed a more precise method of determining time than given by Moon, which varies the time of Her cycles from year to year. So they became astronomers, turning to the more predictable Sun to precisely identify key points of the year—the Solstices (longest and shortest day—June 21 and Dec. 21) and Equinoxes (the spring and autumn dates—March 21 and Sept. 21—which have day and night of equal length and lay midway between Solstice and Equinox). They are the cornerposts upon which the solar calendar is based and are high sacred feast days. The solstices, in particular, are regarded because they symbolize and epitomize the eternal cycle of renewal.

The farther north an agricultural People lives, the greater the role of the Solstices in their life and ritual. The contrast in day length between summer and winter Solstice is more extreme the farther north one goes, as are the extremes of the seasons. The shorter growing season gives greater importance to accurately determining the times for various crop-related activities. The climatic extremes also affect nonagricultural involvements to a greater degree in the warm Moons, emphasis is placed upon food storage, with summer and winter diets varying considerably. Winter affords more time for craftwork, and feasts and ceremonies.

In the North Country, a person's age is counted by the passing winters. The White Season is a time of creativity and introspection, when more time is spent indoors—a symbolic returning to the womb. So the passing of winter is a rebirthing as one comes out again to greet the new cycle. This season can also be a critical one for the young, sick, and aged, so its passing is a milestone to remember and recount.

So the Lunar cycle came to be of secondary importance with agriculturists. Similarly, the Solar cycle is secondary with the primarily nonagricultural Old Way Peoples. Their astronomy usually does not identify the Solstices and Equinoxes, and they are seldom commemorated. Time as it relates to the Lunar cycle has a more direct bearing on the rhythms of their lives, which are more generally seasonal, and more in line with the big sweeps of time that coincide with the Mooncycles.

Moon cycles (referred to simply as "Moons" by Old Way People) are identified by the primary activities or seasonal changes that they encompass. The names of individual Moons vary according to region and culture. Following are the Moons as we know them here in the Northern Forest. They speak of a life in which time passes gently from one season and activity to another, and of a life Walked close to its essence, its spirit.

    January — Snow Moon, Spirit Moon
    February — Hunger Moon, Sucker Spawning Moon
    March — Crust on Snow Moon, Raven Awakening Moon
    April — Sap Boiling Moon, Wild Goose Moon
    May — Flower (Budding) Moon, Planting Moon
    June — Strawberry Moon, Wild Rose Moon
    July — Blueberry Moon, Thunder Moon
    August — Raspberry Moon, Green Corn Moon
    September — Wild Rice Moon, Harvest Moon
    October — Falling Leaves Moon, Hunter's Moon
    November — Freezing Over Moon, Beaver Moon
    December — Long Night Moon, Little Spirit Moon

As already mentioned, the relationship between the Gregorian months and their corresponding Moons is only approximate. This is because Moons, which average 29 ½ days in length, are generally a day or so shorter than months. Thus, within a Solar year, twelve Moons will have missed filling a Solar year by about ten days. The next year's Moons will then occur about ten days earlier. The following chart illustrates this; it gives the dates of the Moons (which run from New Moon to New Moon) for four consecutive years.

1994	1995	1996	1997
1/11	1/01		
2/10	1/30	1/20	1/09
3/12	3/01	2/18	2/07
4/10	3/30	3/19	3/09
5/10	4/29	4/17	4/07
6/09	5/29	5/17	5/06
7/08	6/27	6/16	6/05
8/07	7/27	7/15	7/04
9/05	8/25	8/14	8/03
10/04	9/24	9/12	9/01
11/03	10/23	10/12	10/01
12/02	11/22	11/11	10/31
	12/21	12/10	11/30
			12/29

After three years, Moons are occuring about 30 days earlier, placing them within the time of the previous Moon. They then take on the previous Moon's name. For example, the Long Night Moon (the last '94 entry above), which begins on 12/2 in 1994 begins on 10/31 in 1997—the time of freezing over. It thus becomes known as the Freezing Over Moon.

Thus every third year (as in 1995) has an extra Moon (similar to the Solar year's extra day every four years). This theoretically extra unnamed Moon actually never shows up because the naming of a Moon is arbitrary and dependent upon what actually occurs within that Moon. For instance, if a particular White Season is long-lived, the Crust on Snow Moon may extend itself to two Moons, or during a warm Autumn the Freezing Over Moon may occur later than normal, overlapping the Long Night Moon. A year may also have a special Moon, such as a Flood Moon to commemorate an uncommonly wet period.

Moon's Cycle

We're now going to follow Moon's path through the Sky and the seasons, so that we can better know Her effect upon us and begin a closer relationship with Her.

The charts below show the yearly rise and set cycles of New Moon (called Dead Moon or Sleeping Moon by some Native Peoples) and Full, or Pregnant, Moon. New Moon is overhead, and strongest, at about midday, and Full Moon is at Her peak at around midnight. In mid-summer New Moon is with us for the longest—16 ½ hours, rising at 4:00 AM and setting at 8:30 PM; Her visits are shortest in mid-winter—8 ½ hours, when She rises at 7:00 AM and sets at 3:30 PM. Full Moon is the opposite; Her midsummer visits are shortest—7 ½ hours, from 8:00 PM to 3:30 AM, and Her mid-winter visits are longest—15 ½ hours, from 4:00 PM to 7:30 AM. (These times are estimates; they will vary slightly depending on locale, but are generally applicable to most of North America and Europe. They do not reflect daylight savings time.) See charts on pages 63 and 64.

As Moon goes through Her cycle, She rises and sets from 20 to 80 minutes later each day. By the time She completes one cycle, this time loss amounts to a whole day. So in a 30 day cycle, She rises and sets only 29 times.

When She rises, She often appears to be larger than normal; this is an illusion popularly attributed to atmospheric magnification. Moon is actually no bigger to the eye at the horizon than She is at Her zenith. She appears larger as She rises because the horizon diminishes her background sky and gives the eye a plane of reference; She appears smaller when risen because She loses Herself in the vastness of the Sky.

Waxing is the term used to designate Moon in the first, or growing, half of Her cycle, from New to Full; *waning* is Her shrinking second half, from Full back to New. The waxing Moon is lit on the right (west) side, the waning Moon is lit on Her left (east) side. I remember the difference by thinking of waxing Moon as walking the Suntrail westward and gaining power and momentum by being increasingly lit each night by setting Sun, whereas waning Moon is facing east, contrary to the Suntrail, so loses a bit of Her light each night.

Our Moon Cycle

Following are some exercises we can do on a daily basis to help bring Moon alive within us. They will also help us to better know the animal and plant brothers and sisters we'll be meeting in Book III, because the patterns and movements of their lives are based on the same Lunar cycles:

— Use Moon as a practical calendar. Keep track of personal dates with Lunar time and use it when talking with like-minded friends. Date letters with the Lunar day. For example, if I was to date this page today, it would be: Hunger Moon, 2nd day past Dead Moon.

— Observe and record Moon's activities for one full cycle—the times of Her rising and setting, when Full, New, and Half, how many days She appears full. At the end of Her cycle, notice the pattern in rising and setting times.

— On the chart on pages 66-67, record your basal body temperature upon rising each day. Do so when first waking up and before getting out of bed, because temperature rises as soon as physical activity commences. Women: day 1 of cycle is the first day of your Moontime (menses). Men: day 1 of cycle is the same as your mate's. If single, day 1 is whatever day you begin recording your temperature. After a few months, the first day of your Moon cycle will become evident. (Body temperatures usually fall within the range of 97-99° F. If higher, one is possibly not in good health; if lower, one's normal temperature could fall below the average range.)

— Each evening, plot your general physical and emotional level for the day, and, if there was anything of note about the way you felt, jot down a few words to describe it on the *comments* line. Record Moon's four major phases (◗ = First Quarter, ○ = Full Moon, ◖ = Last Quarter, ● = New Moon). At the end of the Moon cycle, compare the pattern of your cycles with that of Moon and see if there are any parallels. Compare your unfolding physical/emotional cycle with your Moontime cycle. Patterns will likely become evident once you have a few cycles' charts to compare. Which points in your cycle do you feel are your best and worst times to make decisions ... your most creative time ... the time in which you tend most toward depression or euphoria?

Notice that the effect of New Moon is much more subtle than that of Full Moon; we have to be sensitively attuned to ourselves in order to recognize it. Some of us who think we feel New Moon are probably actually experiencing a state devoid of Full Moon effect.

Surprising to many, men have Moon cycles also. Their basal temperatures and energies fluctuate just as women's, but not as dramatically. When a man and woman are close, their Moon patterns fall into sync.

Elders
   Two books that offer good guidelines on taking your basal temperature:
Margaret Nofziger, *A Cooperative Method of Natural Birth Control*
Art Rosenblum, *The Natural Birth Control Book*
   For a wealth of information on Moon's physics, geography, tides, eclipses, etc.:
Kim Long, *The Moon Book*

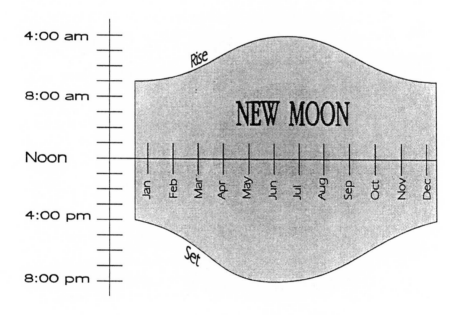

Chart 1. New Moon Yearly Rise and Set Cycle

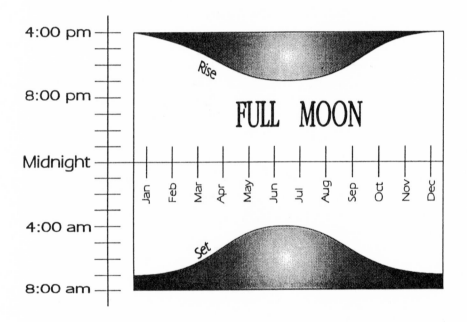

Chart 2. Full Moon Yearly Rise and Set Cycle

Some regular calendars also incorporate the Lunar calendar and can be useful, especially at the beginning of our reaquaintanceship. However, those calendars that list Moon's phases as FQ or First Quarter and LQ or Last Quarter can be misleading, as the quarter referred to is a quarter cycle; Moon is actually half-full.

There are two good Lunar calendars available in bookstores or by mail order. Though dissimilar in format, they're both well executed and make useful companions. They each show Moon as She would appear each day, accompanied for reference by the Gregorian date and day of week. Luna Press's is laid out as is a standard calendar and includes Her rising, setting, and astrological times, Celtic symbolism, and complementary poetry and artwork. The Johnson Books version is in poster form. Although it doesn't contain as much information as Luna's, it makes it possible to view the whole Lunar year at a glance. Order them from:

Johnson Books
1880 So. 57th Court
Boulder, CO 80301

Luna Press
Box 511, Kenmore Station
Boston, MA 02215

The Moment

"Time is yours," said Talks With Loons as she read the exasperated expression on my face. We had made plans to meet at a predesignated campsite, and she arrived an hour or so after I expected her. I had grown increasingly frustrated and impatient as I waited.

"Even though I wasn't here, you were giving your time to me. In doing so, you were giving away your Power; your preoccupation with my arrival stole your sense of self. The future became your dwelling place, your seat of Power. Your strained and hopeful visions of my arrival flooded your present, washing away the precious moment in which you dwell."

That was many years ago, but I still remember like it was yesterday how awkward I felt as Talks With Loons' words framed my state of being. Each word made me feel more like a sore thumb in relation to my surroundings. For that entire hour while I waited for her, everything around me screamed the moment's bliss, and I was too numb, too wrapped up in my own time-concept to hear it.

Terms like "Sun time", "Indian time", and "woods time" are used as a joking reference to the time system of some people who are habitually late. But what actually is this implied atypical sense of time? A Native in the Civilized world, the precision black-and-white world of absolutes, is like

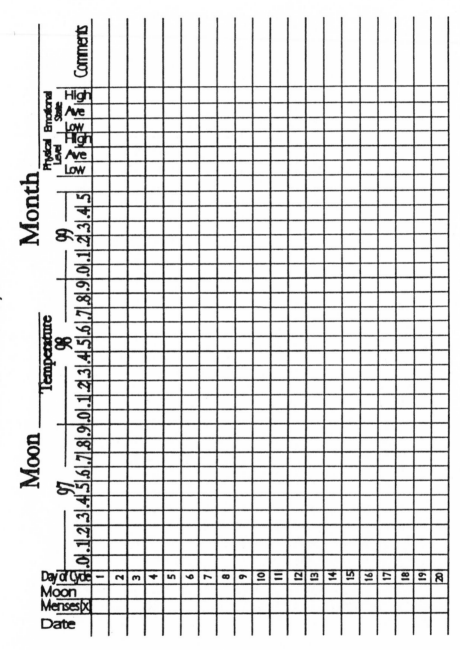

Personal Mooncycle Chart

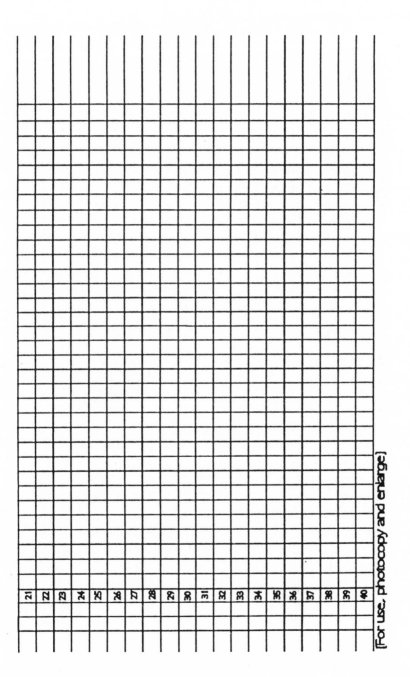

[For use, photocopy and enlarge]

Chart 3. Personal Mooncycle Chart

a fish out of water. Living on the bosom of The Mother is dwelling in a world of ebb and flow, of unexpecteds and relativisms that don't lend themselves well to time in a box. For example, if a woman tells a man that she will meet him at some particular place at some time of day, say late afternoon, there is either an implied or stated suffix in reference to her time of arrival that means "or thereabouts." This concept of nonpunctuality is understood by all Old Way People, but it is sometimes stated anyway as a courtesy.

She will most likely leave early for the meeting place, so that she'll have time for the inevitable but unforeseen. Perhaps she'll meet a clanswoman on the trail who could use some help with an unexpectedly large picking of berries, or she may come across a family of playing Otters and spend some time watching them. Whatever it is, she can immerse herself in it without having to suffer the anxiety of possibly being late.

If he arrives first, he may hunt a Grouse and dig up some Leeks for the evening meal or use the time to practice a skill. He is living his life, regardless of when or if she arrives, and he knows that she is doing the same, so he has no cause to smoulder in anticipation. Whoever arrives first will greet the other with friendliness, as his (or her) time has been passed in the fullness of the moment, without concern for who arrives first or second.

Being in the moment comes from being in a state of harmonious and spontaneous Balance, as in the above example. This, and this only, brings happiness. Thoughts, which are based on past experiences, can bring on pleasant feelings, as can visions of future possibilities. Pleasant feelings are not happiness. To create pleasant feelings one has to think, to conjure; to be in a state of happiness one merely has to be.

The Path to Balance is being ever aware of what is real and what isn't. What isn't lies in the realm of memory-based thought and projection—past and future dwelling. What is real is the moment, free of judgement, guilt, expectation, or insecurity. These feelings are based on comparing past memory or future projection with the present. They are memory-based, so have nothing to do with the moment's reality. Because change is ever occurring, comparisons of past and possible future to present are irrelevant. The past no longer exists, and our memory of it is subjectively selective, so it is not a valid basis for our feelings about the moment. And the future does not yet exist, so neither does it have a bearing on our present feelings.

Native People have no words for comparing past thoughts or future projections with the present—no parallels for the Civilized *should*, *could*, *ought, might, ideal*. They are a People who live in the now—the only shared reality, the only reality that brings us into Oneness with the Greater Circle. They have a past and they recognize a future, but immersion in the moment's lushness does not allow either of them to alter or negate or justify the ongoing experience. They own their feelings; they haven't enslaved them to the past or sold them to the future. Happiness—pure, unadorned, and unencumbered—is intrinsic to the Path they walk, and to the Path of all who Walk the Old Way in the various realms and kingdoms.

Time

Time does not exist. We create it by developing a tension between past and future, then sitting between the two. The ongoing process of life is then either drawn fore or aft by the tension, causing the process to more resemble a product, an end. If drawn fore it becomes a goal, an ideal; if drawn aft it becomes a regret, a debt to pay. Our self-imposed bleeding of the present strips us of the full experience and sensation of life as it is given to us. We lose our innate awareness that the process *is* the product, that the beauty of life *is* in its living.

If we were truly rational beings, we would know that the present very quickly becomes the past and the future can only be lived in the present. So being immersed in the moment and true to that moment is the way to create a past without misgivings and a future without anxiety.

We Humans are the only people who have evolved a concept of time. Perhaps we did it as a way to try to get a grasp on fear. Fear of the unknown is actually fear of the future, and fear based upon experience is fear of the past. The concept of time gives us access to the future and past so that we can deal with our fears. Now we are on a time treadmill that is hard to step off of: trying to reshape the past and preshape the future so that we have nothing to fear aborts fulfillment of the moment. This spoiled moment soon becomes a past of regret and flat memory and quickly taints our future by sending us into the next moment not fully conscious or involved. As we keep stepping hollowly into the next moments, which quickly become our stale present and shapeless past, we begin a series of time overlays that perpetuate themselves and wrap us into a Circle without end.

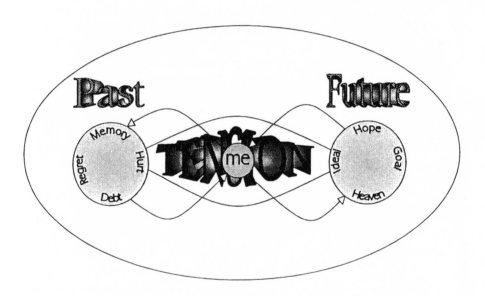

Chart 4. Time-Tension

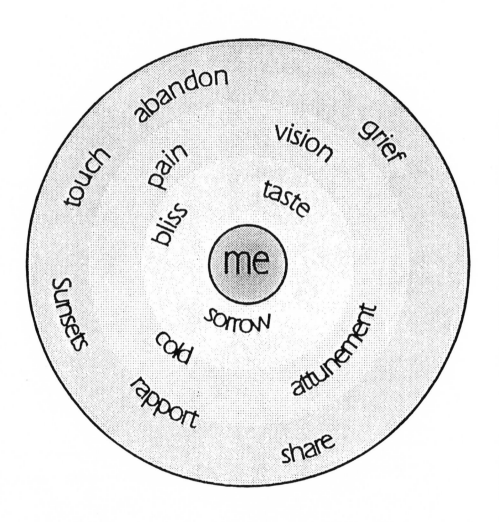

Chart 5. Time-Immersion

Speed

Time has an aspect—*speed*—which is relative to each situation and each of our individual perspectives. An event occurring within a year's time can be fast for one person, and the same event happening within a day can be slow for another. So when we have some effect on time as it touches someone who is caught in its grip, we are respectful of that person if we step back and allow speed its sway. Not having power over the pace of time can be extremely stressful and repressive. Slowing a person can put a constraint on her personal unfolding, and forcing a person might propel her at an uncomfortable pace.

As we become more attuned to the moment and time becomes less a master, speed also loses its relevance. Fast becomes slow, slow becomes fast, and, in the ultimate, night becomes day and life becomes death becomes life. All exist synchronously, one evolving from the other, and one becoming the other. Then things become as they are, as they are intended to be. We let go of trying to make them as we wish them to be, or to perceive them as they are not. We let things happen as they will and find bliss in their unfoldment.

Some of what we are sharing may not make a whole lot of sense to you at this time, and indeed, I do not fully comprehend its depths and fringes myself. If a pitiful Journeyer like me was deemed worthy of these wisdoms and taken as a hopeful candidate, then I'm sure it is more than equally possible for you. I give these glimpses of what we are growing toward because that is what was done with me, so that I could recognize it when I came to it, and so that I would already have a closet in which to hang the new garments of awareness as they came to me.

There is an old maxim which states, "Know your enemy if you wish to conquer it." We have begun, but time is a powerful enemy, so there is much we need to know. Growth through time takes time. It is part of the Journey.

Deep Time

There is another form of time that we wish to encourage instead of diminish, called *Deep Time*. Our Ancestors speak to us in Deep Time, and it is in Deep Time that Vision comes to us. In the same way that an orgasm cannot be given in words, there is no way of adequately describing Deep Time. An effort at such could at best dance around it yet perhaps risk bruising with expectation and preconception the realm from which Deep Time comes to us.

Deep Time is akin to a dimension that exists parallel to ours, in which the more ethereal forces of life walk beside us. These spirit-forces are actually with us, but we are not conscious of their presence when we dwell in regular time, because the two times are not synchronous. When we Quest for Vision or enter dreamtime, our main task is to put time aside so that we can enter Deep Time. It is there that we can converse with the Ancestors and become the embodiment of our Dodem (the bird, fish, plant, etc., who has the same spirit as we do, and who has come to us and offered to be our Guardian and empowerment).

The rhythm of Soft Drumming (see Drum chapter in Book II) can help create a compatable bridge to draw us over into Deep Time.

While walking in Deep Time, one can be attuned to the normal world, but while walking in the normal world, one cannot be attuned to Deep Time. In my travels I have met and shared with only one person who is an exception; he walks with the feet and eyes of his Dodem and has the Ancestors as his constant companions. He has been long on his Journey and has found the place where time does not exist. I am blessed for being guided to him, because he gave me the vision of that place beyond the Veil, so that someday I may lift it as well. Then perhaps I can repay the Blessing by gifting it to others.

I am told there are more people like him, most of whom now live in the few Sacred Places where our kind still honor The Mother by Walking the Old Way.

Elder
Robert H. Merrill, *The Calendar Stick of Tshi-zun-hau-kau*

The voicings of the insects, the birds, and the Water
contribute their sounds . . . like Goo koo koo — Ojibway for Owl.

Earth Language

Gayigwa nayab agimadabid a Makwa iwa Saga'igan babamagamad. A Mishgwadasi owabaman babamagogamanid inandam Mishgwadasi: "Wi'kaga, daba'kubi!"

In a while back out on the Lake came Bear, wandering about upon the shore. Painted Turtle saw him roaming about on the shore. Thought Painted Turtle: "Oh, let him go into the Water!"

—example of the Algonquian dialect—spoken by the Ojibway (or Chippewa)—the Upper Great Lakes Natives who call themselves Nishinabeg.

Several years ago a chance word association gave me a lesson in how a language can store relics of its culture's ceremonial past: My blood family colloquially uses the word noggin in reference to one's head or skull; Algonquian People use the term to refer to a cup or bowl. Knowing that skulls are sometimes used as bowls by Old Way People—especially ceremonially, I realized that what I stumbled upon may not have been just chance similarity.

My mother thought the word came from the German side of the family. That's all the incentive I needed to delve into the mystery, as I was already aware of the mounting evidence (linguistic and otherwise) pointing to an early Norse (a Germanic People)—Algonquian association.

English linguists aren't sure of the origin of the term, speculating that it probably came from nog—an old Angle (a Germanic People inhabiting England) word referring to a mug and the ale that was drunk from it.

In contemporary English usage, noggin means either a mug, a unit of liquid measure, or a person's head. Being also a unit of measure (probably deriving from the fact that drink was charged for by the mug), I speculated that if the Algonquian and German words were of the same origin, they would be found in both languages also as relating to trade. (Trade terms are usually the first elements of language exchange.) Sure enough, I found the Algonquian term noggima, which means to put a price on something.

Knowing what I do of the cultural-spiritual kinship of the Algonquian and Norse, I suspect that the Skull Noggin was shared amongst them in the Circle of Ceremony as well as in the Circle of trade.

Living Tongues

It is commonly said that in order to know a People, one must know their language. To that I would like to add my feeling that in order to know The

Earth, one must know a language spoken by Earth People. When Natives have lived in an area since a time that only legends can recount, their language takes on the character of the land. The voicings of the insects, the birds, and the Water contribute their sounds, and the spirit and tempo of the locale lend their rhythm. Grammatical structure and how the language is used as a component of communication are influenced by the way the plants and animals communicate, actually contributing many words directly to the language. It is a *living language*—a part of the total language of The Earth.

The language common to all of Creation is the language of the spirit and of the heart. It is a language unbounded by words and rational-linear concepts, so it easily transcends the barriers of culture and species. It is often the language we attempt to use when we choose words and realize that our words are saying more than we intend, or something other than what we intend. Usually it is our feelings and intuitions we wish to share rather than the message our words give.

Civilized People stretch the limits of verbage in this way because they have forgotten that the majority of communication is nonverbal. Their emphasis on words gives them a frail and inadequate means of communication. Whereas Old Way People use individual words more conceptually, Civilized People define their terms more narrowly and categorically. For example, Civilized People would take many words to convey the concepts of Circle, Time, and Moon, while Natives have this information available to them through other than verbal means.

The advent of the written language, and now the recorded language, has taken communication another step away from spirit communion and has left it even more one-dimensional. Effective, fully expressive communication depends considerably on facial expression, gestures, tone and volume, smell, and the dynamic created by their interplay. (There is an African People who don't feel comfortable talking with people unless they are close enough to be smelled.)

The Other Voice of Language

Language can also be a sharing of another sort; besides being the spoken word of its People, it tells of their origins and traditions. Culture may change, but language, being highly structured, persists. When one People merges with another, they quite easily adopt a common lifeway, but they choose one or the other of their languages as the common tongue.

The Navajo are a good example of the strength of language over culture: they were a nomadic Apache People who migrated down from the North, adopted the sedentary, agricultural pueblo life of their new neighbors but retained their own language.

When Peoples of differing languages come together for trade or counsel, the same generalization applies—one of their languages will be chosen as the "shared" tongue.

The English language speaks of its People's origins and traditions in a slightly different way. It is a bastard language—clearly that of an assimilative soldiering and merchanting People. Just as the growth of its civilization fed on the spoils of war and attrition, trade, and genocide, so did its language.

Being so plastic and changeable, English, unlike the typical Native language, is a muddy and complex chronicle of the origins of its speakers and their culture. To its Germanic base has been added chunks and tidbits from the languages of the conquering and the conquered. We find a major dose of Latin structure, Greco-Roman technical terms and word roots, French everyday words, and a smattering of words from dozens of other sources.

Because English is comprised primarily of nonEnglish and archaic Germanic words, it is no longer a living language. Its words must be learned by intellectual association, whereas in living languages words are descriptive of what they represent.

For example, the word *Birch* means nothing to us in and of itself until we are shown what to associate it with. In a typical Native language the Birch would be called something akin to "tree with curling white bark." In fact, to the speakers of the old Germanic tongue from which *Birch* came, it meant exactly that. It was self-descriptive; no intellectual association had to be made.

There are some recently-evolved English words that are similar to what would be commonly found in a living language, such as *Rattlesnake* and *Red-Winged Blackbird*.

Another characteristic of a living language is that it has a good proportion of words that have a phonetic association with what they represent. This can occur in two ways: The word can convey an impression or feeling for its namesake, such as the Ojibway term for bog—*Mushkeg*. Or the word can derive from the sound that something makes, like *Goo koo koo*—Ojibway for Owl. Similarly, *Oolool* was the original English word for Owl before it took its present form. *Swish* and *moan* are two contemporary English examples.

Nouns, adjectives, and adverbs predominate in the Civilized languages, whereas the living tongues are comprised mainly of verbs; they are languages of flow. Even a good share of their nouns are derived from, or transformed into, verbs.

In the living languages, nouns and verbs are usually not used alone; adjectives and adverbs (the qualifying and descriptive words that are associated with nouns and verbs) are an intrinsic part of the words. Without these modifiers, noun and verb roots could be next to meaningless. For example, the Inuit have terms for many different types of snow, but not one that refers just to generic snow.

In general, the degree to which nouns and verbs of a language are descriptive unto themselves is indicative of the degree to which its speakers Walk the Old Way. (This is not true of People newly civilized or newly returning to The Earth, because, as discussed earlier, language persists in the face of change.)

Adjectives in the Civilized languages are usually abstract and bear no direct relation to their object except by association. In English, for instance, the adjective *cold* can be used in association with any number of nouns, whereas in Native languages there are usually a number of specific terms to indicate cold in relation to specific nouns or situations.

In the Civilized languages, the *subject* of the sentence usually appears first, as in, "*I* made Venison stew." Whereas in the Native languages, the *object* of the sentence usually appears first, as in "*Venison stew* was made by me."

Subject-first sentence structure is found mainly in Civilized languages, whose speakers tend to see themselves as the Glory of Creation. This causes their lifeways to tend toward narcissism (people-centeredness). Their speech patterns, reflecting that focus, are based on subject (which is often people) emphasis.

Object-first structure allows for more intimate, less intellectually-based involvement by the listener. Whereas, the subject-first sentence structure requires the speaker to place more emphasis on self or other people than the object.

In the object-last sentence, "I saw a big, beautiful, ancient, leaning *tree*," the listener does not know what is being described until the very last word, so she must remain intellectually keyed in to the speaker, preventing her from getting personally involved in the word-picture he is painting.

There is a very practical reason for object-first sentence structure in an immersion/now-centered lifeway—the need for focus and involvement over the need for abstraction and intellectualization. For example, if you and I were hunting and you saw a Deer up ahead, you would first want to direct my attention toward the Deer before discussing stalking strategy.

Native People are not prone to think in absolutist terms. The awareness that things are not always as they seem is reflected in their speech; they leave room for other possibilities. A couple of statements illustrating this would be: "Moon Hawk left for the Cranberry Lake last night, I think," and "Grandmother died in her sleep last night, perhaps." Likewise, Native nouns tend to be less blunt and categorical (pigeonholing) than Civilized nouns.

In most of the Civilized languages, pronouns are either masculine or feminine. When a pronoun is needed, one or the other must be chosen, whether or not the sex of the person(s) is known, and generally the masculine pronoun is used. A similar situation exists with words like postman, chairman, etc. Sometimes the implied or selected gender is appropriate, and sometimes it is insensitive to the need for a reference that is sexless, beyond sex, or encompasses both sexes. In spite of the contemporary awareness and emphasis placed upon this issue, I have yet to find an alternative that is not awkward or alienating. Attempts at sensitizing the Civilized languages seem about as successful as painting a smile on a Piranha.

In some Native languages, some pronouns can refer to either gender. They are used out of respect, to be sure to include everyone and not to embarrass anyone if the gender isn't known. (This is an example of the nonabsolutist, less categorical characteristics just discussed. Sometimes the pronoun is nothing more than a suffix of the verb, which refers back to the noun. The suffix cannot stand alone as a pronoun, so it implies no gender other than that of the noun.

Generally speaking, the living languages treat elements of Earth as feminine, elements of Sky as masculine, and elements of Spirit with no gender connotation.

Speaking Life

I am learning the Native language of my area because I want to speak and think and sing in the living tongue born of The Mother on which I walk. I want the Birds and the Grasses to hear my words as they would hear the crackling Frost and the talking Stream; I want the Hills to befriend me as a speaker of the sweet language they have echoed for untold generations of its speakers. I want to honor life in words that speak life; I want my family to share the beauty within these words and the wisdoms that come through them with words that know how to respect and express such voicings.

The sounds of my adopted tongue touch like familiar poetry, perhaps because my Old Way kin from long ago and over the Ocean came here and left a trace of their voice for me now to hear. I have already been greatly blessed by the guidance of my new language; as I studied her, she gifted me with much of what I have learned about time and prayer and how to Walk.

Elders
Barry Fell, *America B.C., Bronze Age America, Saga America*
J.W. Powell, *Indian Linguistic Families*
Reider Sherwin, *The Viking and the Red Man*, Vols. I-VIII
Carl F. Voegelin, *Map of North American Indian Languages*
    (1966, American Ethnologial Society)
Willard Walker, *The Proto-Algonquians* (from *Linguistics and Anthropology*, by
    Kinkade, Hale, and Werner)
Benjamin Lee Whorf, *Language Thought and Reality*

III

People of the Old Way

. . . I recognize the land upon which I walk as still being under their caretakership.

Introduction to Part III

Now we'll meet on a more personal level those People whose ways and spirit we have begun to know. Until now I've shied away from getting specific about who these People are, so that we could first grow in awareness that they—no matter what their name or distinction, no matter which region of The Mother they call home, and no matter what their color or culture or language—are all Native Earth People, all sharing the same lifeway. And I did it so that we could identify with these People as being us—us in a different cloak and a different time. Now I'm going to bring it closer to home by beginning with the Old Way People most of us are best acquainted with—the North American Natives.

Clans and Conquerors

Let's start with Columbus, as the era of colonialism he symbolically kicked off is the primary reason for you and me being here and Walking these pages together. It is popularly held that this continent's People were first called Indians because Colombus believed that he had reached India. Recent research is indicating that he knew full well where he was going, and it wasn't India.

Columbus used the story of seeking a new route to the East as a guise to obtain sponsorship for his voyage. He spent years researching old nautical charts and interviewing seasoned sailors in Mediterranean port towns. They told him tales of the land that lay to the west (America), which were passed down from their predecessors who had been there.

Parts of Columbus's nautical charts and log don't make sense to historians, because they seem inconsistent with the then-current knowledge of navigation and geography. Viewed in light of his prior knowledge of the Americas, his records clearly indicate that was his destination.

The term *Indian* was probably not applied to the American Natives because of mistaken identity, as India was not known as such at the time, but as Hindustan and Pakistan. More likely, the term came from the Spanish "una gente en Dios," which means, "a People in God". To those who later followed Columbus and wanted to believe that his discovery was a route to India (as the country by then became known), En Dios sounded close enough to India that they began calling the Natives "Indians. (Columbus inspired the reference "una gente en Dios" when he said of his first meeting with the Natives, "In the world, there is not a better nation. They love their neighbors as themselves, and their discourse is ever sweet and gentle.")

The concept of the "Indian" as a distinct people, or race, originated with the Conquerors and was promulgated by them to the point that now even the Natives see themselves as such. The Church saw them as heathens ripe for "The Word," as unwitting victims in the unrolling of Divine Destiny— the inevitable, God-patterned plan of human events. These rationales, along with the Civilized concept of race, made it convenient to view all of the Native inhabitants as the same and group them under the label "Indian."

The Natives saw and see themselves quite differently; the Yaqui call themselves *Yoemen*, the Pima know themselves as *O-otam*, the Apache are *N'de*, *Tsistsista* is the Cheyenne name for themselves, and the Ojibway refer to themelves as *Nishnabe*—all of which mean "The People." They view themselves each as nations and cultural entities unto themselves.

Most of the present tribal names originated as references made by the Conquerors or by neighboring tribes. For instance, the Nishinabeg (Ojibway) referred to their enemies to the west as Snakes, or *Nadowesiw*, which the French transcribed as "Sioux." The Ojibway, in their own language, referred to their kin to the south as *Menominee*, or Wild Rice People. These references were adopted as the official tribal names by the government and eventually accepted by the tribes as well.

Tribes as we know them today did not exist prior to the Conquerors' contact. Banding together for defense and the imposed regimen of the reservation encouraged related Peoples to assume a tribal identity. These hunting-gathering Peoples were originally organized around extended family units, or Clans, named after their Guardian Beings, or Dodems (Totems). They are usually mammals and birds, but other animals such as insects, plants, inanimate objects, and etherial entities can also be Dodems. Clans of the same culture had loose associations that brought them together periodically for trade and ceremony.

Specialized crafts and services available only outside of one's Clan were arranged for at these gatherings. They also served as meeting-places for potential mates, as tradition held that they be sought outside of one's own Clan.

The People identified strongly with their Clan and its Dodem. When visiting another band of the same Clan, they would be treated as one of their own, as close blood relation, even though they may be total strangers. A Dodem was esteemed and honored as the Guardian of its People and was looked upon for inspiration and guidance. The People would emulate their Dodem by observing his ways and adapting them to their lives.

Clan structure and Clan ways have largely disintegrated under the new cloak of tribal identity. Along with them has gone much of the beauty of the Old Way, as tribal structure, because of its size and political realities, does not allow for the diversity in lifeway and expression of the Clan system that so enriched and empowered the People.

Grouping these diverse Clan Peoples together as a race called Indian is a misrepresentation of reality and a belittling of the people it affects. Official policy and popular conception, aided by the media and ease of travel, are creating a people to fit the mold—a Pan-Indian culture is evolving. Christianity has lent a commonality to Native spirituality, and the Bureau of Indian Affairs (BIA) has given it political uniformity. The corrals given them for homelands and the plow and the Cow given them in place of their communion with The Mother have given them common problems. Pow-wows now replace the gathering of Clans for ceremony and trade, and there are "top ten" songs that roll off of Drums from Ocean to Ocean.

In the Old Way, one is of The People if she lives as The People. If a daughter chooses to live differently, she is no longer of The People. If a man from another world chooses to live as The People, he is a brother. The BIA now recognizes standards to determine who is or is not of The People. Blood standards. Generally, if one is ¼ Blood or more, one is eligible to be registered on the tribal rolls and be *of* The People. If one is less than ¼ Blood, one is not *of* The People.

At least on the surface, the Conquerors have succeeded in luring and prodding these Clanspeople into the mold every Conqueror desires—a caged, isolated, easily identifiable minority.

On the reservations, the Old Way fades further as bitterness, frustration, and confusion set in. This climate has drawn a number of their People to adopt some of the standards and characteristics of their oppressors: on occasion those of mixed ancestry are discriminated against, and "non-Indians" are sometimes threatened with violence. Some Native radicals say that they are of the Chosen Race—that the old Medicine Way is theirs only, by right of Blood. In some areas the Guidings and Medicine of their Elders are no longer easily available to those from outside who Seek.

She Who Talks With Loons has told me that when folks share with her their wish to become as Indians, she seldom says anything. She feels that it is not her place to tell them that the Indian they envision is in part an invention of, and a reaction to, the dominant Culture, and that the Indian they seek is already within them. This knowledge and awareness comes and fits better, she says, if they arrive at it on their own, as that is the way it will speak most truthfully to their yearning.

Tribal Wars

The history books of my upbringing dealt smugly with the issue of inter-tribal friction. We were left with the impression that war was the normal state of affairs for these Peoples, as we were given no insight into the cause-and-effect relationship of these frictions or the broader political backdrop.

In actuality, the various Peoples lived largely in a state of balance amongst themselves prior to colonial times and were mostly sedentary. The tension caused by Civilized expansionism, economic disruption, and the imbalances created by the acquisition of guns and the Horse brought on the bloody, nomadic ways that we were led to believe as being the norm for these Peoples.

A prime example is the untold story of the great migrations of the Northeastern Forest: colonial pressure and fur lust encouraged Iroquois movement, which put them at odds with their Algonquian neighbors, in turn hastening Algonquian westward migration. The Ojibway—the Algonquian group in the forefront of the migration, moved into the region of Lake Superior and the upper Mississippi—the historical homeland of the Lakota (Sioux).

In pre-Civilized times, the Lakota were Woodland dwellers; those living on the Prairie fringe ventured out to hunt the migrating Buffalo when they came close to the Forest edge. It wasn't until their meeting with the Horse that they moved out onto the Plains en masse, adopted large portable Teepees, and began following Buffalo as a way of life. During this time of the blossoming and flourishing of the Lakota Plains culture, the Ojibway "invaded" (according to the old history books) their lands.

The Ojibway actually found the Woodlands largely uninhabited, as the Lakota had already abandoned the Forest for the Prairie. The Lakota-Ojibway bloodshed came later, after the Ojibway were given the advantage of guns and the Lakota sent war parties back into the Forest in an attempt to maintain equilibrium. The traditional raids—the largely blood-less means for a Warrior to prove dedication and valor, and for a People to seek revenge—became massacres fueled by traders' greed and settlers' plow and saw.

This is but an example of what has been and is repeated everywhere the forces of materialist cultures rub shoulders with the Mother's caretakers. Only recently have I seen that the educational systems of those cultures are beginning to acknowledge and reflect some semblance of actuality in their teachings.

Survival

Recently I heard a local Native woman address the concerns she had for her children being exposed to Civilization's ways, which were in direct contradiction to the ways of her People. Her attempted solution was to teach her culture's values as her children's primary values at home, and, because their culture was immersed in that of the Civilized culture, she would teach that culture's values as tools—survival tools—for their inevitable venturing forth.

This experience has led me to ask if Natives are still of the People when they have been forced to accept the bounds and ownership of a square of Earth, and the guilt and blood-saturated cash of their Conquerors. Or when their children are taken away to schools that teach God from a book and English with a switch, then sent home cold to the ways and language that are the breath and heart of their Ancestors. Or when they break in the face of dictates and bribes to set up governments that usurp the place of the Traditional men and women of wisdom and spirit. Is a Buffalo still a Buffalo when she is corralled and fed hay and no longer has the Wolf and the sweet Grass to keep her lean and healthy?

Some of my answer came in seeing for myself a renewed sense of identity amongst my Native neighbors. Their struggle to maintain and revive their traditional ways is bringing about a rebirth of their culture. The majority consider their old Lifeway to be a thing of the past, their renewed traditions are not necessary as they once were, and no Native People has yet survived the forces of assimilation. Yet there was never a time like this one. Or a crying. Talks With Loons feels that as long as there is life there is hope. . .

Equality and Justice

I've watched a band of Wolves send its most able scout ahead, and upon her return, plan their hunt based upon her valued judgement. And I've seen a scout of the Nettle plants find a new River sandbar that she deemed suitable habitat and then bring the rest of her Clan to join her. Virtually all of the Old Way social plant and animal people I've been honored to live with and observe hold a respect for wisdom that I feel is more functional and nurturing than the Civilized concept of equality.

In the Old Way, equality as an abstract ideal does not exist. When living close to The Mother, individuals, of necessity, function within areas of evolved expertise. The rest of the band gives respect and credence to these people in their specialty areas.

Common examples are the Elders' role as sources of wizened perspective, and grandparents as the acknowledged experts in child rearing. In campsite selection, women and men have complementary roles: women respect the men's awareness of hunting and strategic considerations, and men respect the women's preeminent knowledge in matters of foraging, lodge, and hearth.

Civilized People tend to judge this system as undemocratic, autocratic, and even sexist. A flower looks different from the inside out; their system of governance goes beyond democracy—it is based on trust. And respect. It is functional only within the context of a band of People united by Blood and/or Spirit.

The People judge each other by more than their actions; a person who steals is not necessarily a thief. That person's needs or motives are not known by someone else who has not made the same footprints. When a People sees life in death and hear the wind for who she really is, it is not so surprising that they would look at the actions of their kin with a more seeing eye.

Seldom are their assessments of others infected with the judgementalism and attendant blame, hypocritical perfectionism, and derogatory gossip found so commonly in those of Civilized Peoples. Instead there is an acceptance and encouragement of differing perspectives, which functions within a cultural climate of humor, pride in self-virtue, and eminent respect of others. This encourages self-assessment and self-atonement, and sensitivity to one's effect upon others.

There are no jails or mental institutions. Because of the close-knit, sharing nature of Native groups, the opportunity, as well as the incentive, for harmful acts is slight. Should there be an act of aberrant behavior, there is ready acceptance by its enactor of its being identified as such. And, being true to life in the moment, there is either ready forgiveness or ready punishment.

Peer pressure plays the strongest role in checking minor infringements. In the few cases of necessity, the Warriors may enforce the unwritten codes.

Ostracism is the worst (and most common) punishment to be meeted out for severe offenses, because isolation from all that is meaningful, along with its accompanying shame, is considered to be a fate worse than death. Seldom does it have to be imposed; personal honor and esteemed respect for kin and lifeway usually lead the offender to a shameful self-exile.

As with physical ailments, there is little of the mental disease associated with Civilized cultures. This is partly because living in Balance is healthinducive, and partly because there is room for some of the expression of individuality of perception and Path that the more regimented societies deem inappropriate and categorize as disease. (This diagnosis often serves as a guise for censorship of a real or imagined threat to its necessarily conformist structure.)

Seeds for the Garden

I put considerable spirit and energy into the study of the People of the Old Way and the perpetuation of their cultures. I do so because I recognize the land upon which I walk as still being under their caretakership. I feel that the Conquerors are intruders who, through flagrant excess and cruel torture of The Great Mother and Her children, have rescinded whatever rights and privileges conquership gave them.

The Native People who maintain the Old Ways and those of other origins who choose to stand and walk with them are the People I honor, the People whose customs and lifeway I respect and follow. They know things we have long forgotten; they are a living repository of wisdoms that the Civilized cultures have lost. In this day, healing knowledge, social and political examples, and spiritual insights are being gifted by these People. They are a living example for the wayward cultures striving toward living gently and respectfully; they are a barometer of progress and a source of inspiration; they are schools of living, where some of us go to seek the Elders and hear the Voices. They are our Ancestors personified, and they are each of us, as, in each of them, we can see our full potential realized. The surviving Native cultures are the remnants of Eden. They hold the one realistic promise for life in this despoiled Garden.

Hoop of Life

With his Gull-like coloration and appearance, the male Marsh Hawk would look just as at-home gliding over water as over the waves of Bluestem on the Bracken Prairie near my Lodge. I watched him most of the nesting season, sailing back and forth just above the grasstips in search of morsels for his nest-tending mate and ever-hungry Hawklets. For fear of leading predators to his family, he never visited the nest, which was concealed in the Hummockgrass of a Marsh just to the east of my Lodge. Instead, his discreetly earth-hued mate would fly up to meet him and he would pass his bounty to her in mid-air.

In the days before the Trees greened, they performed their mating dance in the sky above my Lodge. One would follow another as they swooped and rose like riders on a roller-coaster. They sang to each other with liquid, Robin-like voice as they went around and around on an invisible circular track. The abandon of their rolls and gyrations spoke of the bliss of courtship.

As I watched, Raven called, and I knew I was being given a Teaching. The Circle of their ritual skydance, and the Circle of their lives as I watched them over the years, became the unfolding lessons of the Hoop of Life. Before me they lived the Seven Cycles, so that I could know them. In their unfolded wisdom, I found answers to questions concerning my Journey that I did not yet know I had. Whenever I enter the Marsh that was their nestland, I lay down an Offering of Kinnikinick in their Honor.

In the span of our lives, we may enter seven distinct Worlds. Their duration varies with each of us, and some of us do not progress through all of the Worlds, walking our later years as we remain in an earlier World. In the Old Way the Worlds are distinct, and the individual's entering and leaving of each is ritually noted. In the Civilized Way—although the Worlds exist—the boundaries are clouded, as people are not consciously aware of the Seven Worlds. The transitions from one to another are arbitrarily set and standardized and therefore lack in significance and are meekly celebrated. Such practice opens the Hoop of Life to deception, as there are no clear ways to tell who walks which World.

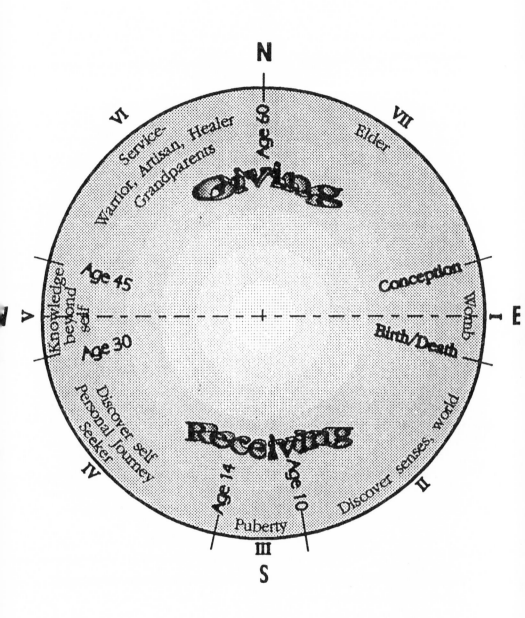

Chart 6. Hoop of Life

The ages noted on the above chart are the average transition ages of Old Way People. The Hoop is divided by a dotted line to signify that in the first several Worlds we are growing and being nurtured, and in later Worlds we nurture and help others to grow. As with all Cirles, Power is given by the Directions they rotate through (see Directions chapter in Book II). East is the direction of beginnings and enlightenment, which is where we die and are born into the Hoop. South is the place of summer growth and innocence, where we, as mature children, briefly spend time, as do caterpillars in their cocoons, and emerge as potentialized adults. In the West is the dwelling place of the Ancestors, where we meet ourselves in their reflection and for the first time are able to read in the etchings of their faces life as it dwells outside and beyond us. North is a quiet place of introspection from which the rest of the Hoop can be observed and relived through the wisdom granted by age and in the time unbounded by one's steps.

The Seven Worlds of the Hoop of Life:

1. Death and Rebirth

Our time in the womb begins as a merging of ancient paths that have died into themselves uncountable numbers of times. Death is a reckoning and purifying process for the Ancestral line, as each time in death the most vibrant and honored part of its life is passed on to the next generation. This process is a continual quest for Balance; the Ancestral line spreads out like an alluvial fan to test its fortunes in various environments and in partnership with other lines. (This is part of the reason for the Journey in World 4.) Birth is nothing more than a continuation in a new environment of the trial marriage of two strings of Ancestors, which began at conception.

2. Body Knowledge

In these several years we are preoccupied with an exploration of our physical self, and of the environment about us, which is also our physical self. (We are a focused concentration of the life of our environment, and our environment's life is a melding of the lives that comprise it.) By exploring, we develop the sensory skills and channels that we will later use in deeper and farther searchings.

3. Puberty

A thirst begins to well up from deep within us, fed by the feeling that we are fast outgrowing our childhood selves, and by the fear of walking beyond childhood. The leisurely pace of our younger years leaves us; we spin in the contradictions of a rapidly constricting shell that forces out the breath of youth and makes it imperative that we quickly look elsewhere for air. In response, the youth turns her back to food and the familiar comforts of lodge, family, and friends and pursues the Dream quest—a solo vigil in anticipation of the revealing of one's Lifepath (see Vision chapter in Book II).

4. Inner Knowledge

We emerge from the Dreamquest feeling awkward and exposed, as our Lifepath has taken on a color and flavor that it has not before worn. The next years are spent wandering and experimenting as we sample those new hues and essences and try to find a niche in which we can display and share them. We are flush with a new sense of self, running the risk of being self-absorbed, headstrong, and unattuned to the voices of wisdom in the reaches beyond us. Contraries (things that appear to be other than what they really are) plague us, making black seem white and giving bite to smiling eyes. It is the time to seek a Guide. By recognizing us as an adult rather than as a daughter or son, our Guide, as an esteemed adult, helps to empower our Lifepath. Our mate does also, for at this time we need emotional nurturing to help sustain our enthusiasm.

5. Circle Knowledge

By about age 30, we have found peace with our Vision. Now we may receive the Gift of Being Nothing (described in the first few pages of this book)—the rite that marks the end of our preoccupation with self. It allows us, for the first time since we have entered puberty, to venture forth and explore the mysteries about us. We travel with a new heart that brings the Song of our Vision to all that we touch. The Elders take new note of us, as it is now that we have the patient time and ears for their sharings. Prior to this, they knowingly sat back and waited, as we were unreachable—our thirst was not for what they had.

6. Sharing Knowledge

It is now that assisting others with that which we have gained on our Journey becomes personally fulfilling. We can fully realize the spirit of giving, gaining fulfillment as others receive. This is the time in which leaders come forth, and artisans and others who serve their People come into their own. It is a stable, involved, and thoughtful realm, in which Personal Power reaches its peak.

7. Sharing Wisdom

Our body slows and we pass our involvements on to those of the prior World as we become more involved in the contemplative state and in dialogue with the Ancestors. It is a time of observation and reflections, a time when we can see ourselves in others to the point where we know their steps, past and future. Our interest in daily events pales to that of the broad sweeps of activity that shape trends and cultures. We share in ways that are oftentimes purposefully subtle and at the same time profound in their emanations. The Elders are the glue that bind as one People those who walk in the various Seven Worlds.

Hoop of Relations

Pigeon is held sacred in the ancient cultures in which he is found. He is likely the first non-Human person to have come live with us, even before Dog. He is unique amongst birds; both male and female produce a milk for their young, and he can drink with a sucking action, not having to tip his head back with each mouthful, as do other birds. Two-thirds of his brain is devoted to his eye, which is more complex than Hawk's. His eye is such a marvel that some speculate that he hears low frequency sounds with it. (The eye and ear are closely related, as they evolved from the same set of nerves.)

I have been honored in being able to live with Pigeons for most of my life. They have shared with me so much of the wisdom of their Ancestral Path that I doubt I would be here writing this book if it were not for them. Through the spirit of Pigeon, I have traveled within the spirit of all birds. As I have looked into his eye to explore its mysteries, I found myself looking outward from within it. From its translucent depths, and through a beauty complex in its resplendency, I began seeing the Circles of my relations in ways that have lent great insight to their place in my life.

I no longer live with Pigeons, but whenever I see one fly, my heart races with him, and I dream of the times I saw through those eyes.

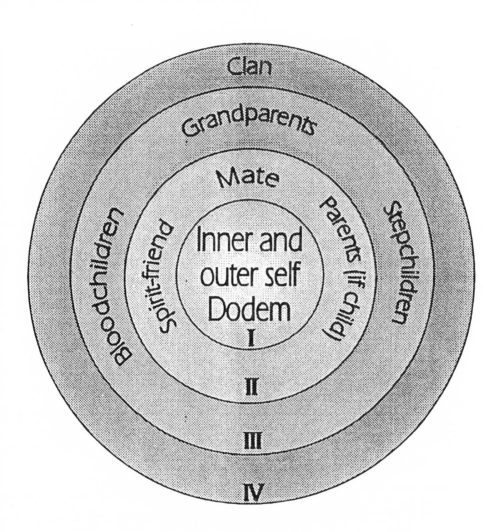

Chart 7. Hoop of Relations

The Four Circles of the Hoop of Relations

1. Self

This is our personal Hoop of Life, centered in its greater context—our Hoop of Relations. I first saw it this way as the pupil of Pigeon's eye:

The Sunlight was reaching deep into the mystery of its inner black reaches, taking me with it. There, within those wondrous microstructures that looked like a queer, tangled Forest on some alien Planet, I found the isolated, dimensionless world I needed to begin grasping who I was in relation to myself. My seat of Power took form from the space within and immediately about me, and I was able to step back and know myself as Pigeon would know the Sky into which he is flying. From thence I gained clear perspective on the People I shared with; I saw them in encompassing Circles as they were related to me (as on the Hoop of Relations illustration).

2. Mate

In the second circle of Pigeon's eye, the iris, is found the eye's character and definition. The same is said by some Elders of us: that the people in our Second Circle—the Circle that immediately surrounds us—give us our character and definition. We can know ourselves and others can know us better by observing those closest to us rather than us directly. This is because we can only see ourselves in reflection. Our view of another is often subjectively guided, so looking at that person's Second Circle gives a variety of reflections to view. The one(s) closest to us, with whom we share bread and heart and spirit, is our Second Circle. The label we may use to identify this person's role in our life is unimportant; it is her/his place at our side that puts her/him there. Having someone in this Circle is essential to our health as social beings. If there is no one there, I do not feel that we can be functioning Humans.

(The outer two Circles, as follows, are not essential to us. There are some for whom one or both do not exist.)

3. Child

We enter this Circle through the one before it, in partnership with the person we walk with in that Circle. Here dwell those with whom we share closely, and who look to us for care. Most often they are our children, but they could be siblings, grandchildren, or any other kin or non-kin who have a relationship with us as would our child. Sometimes our pets dwell in this Circle, especially if it is devoid of our own kind. I know of a few who, given the choice, actually prefer their pets to Human People.

4. Clan

Our three inner Circles rotate within the Circle of all with whom we have more casual relationships. They may be those we spend a lot of time with, such as fellow employees, but we don't share enough with them to bring them in to one of our inner Circles. Or they may be those we feel close to but see so sporadically that we cannot develop an inner Circle relationship with them.

The inner Circle is the most important one in our Hoop of Relations; the Circles decrease in importance as we go out from there. We must be in attunement with the closer Circle in order to be attuned to the one beyond it. For example, if there is family discord, we cannot expect to be well with our children if we are not well with our mate. Our first love and allegiance goes to our mate, because this, in turn, provides the best possible environment for our children.

When we are attuned with Spirit and Balanced within ourselves, we bring Blessings to the Circles around us, which emanate outward in decreasing strength from one to another. And, when we are in such a state, forces that would harm us are diffused. As they work their way inward, they progressively weaken in passing through the ever-stronger influence of our Blessings.

Those who dwell in the three Circles about us are most often of our own kind, but they may also be from the plant and animal Clans. Twenty years ago, when I knew only Civilized People, I asked the Wolves to grace my Hoop of Relations. I preferred Wolves to People at the time; I could sense the integrity and feel the Personal Power of every Wolf I met, whereas the Humans of my culture seemed as pallid as so many domestic Dogs.

I have since grown to know that it was actually myself that I was having trouble with, and not those around me, as many of them, I discovered, were also seeking that which I found in Wolves. Now the non-Human people dwell within my Hoop not because I am running from my kind, but because they have also asked me to dwell within their Hoop.

Life Energy

All that has life is fueled by sexual energy. We are enacting the fertile union of Sun and Earth, continuing the sexual chain reaction they began. Every exchange is sexual—a tentative sharing that might or might not bear fruit. The bringing together of pipestem and bowl is a sexual act, as is the sharing of words with a friend, and the viewing of a bird crossing the sky.

In the following chapters of this section, we are not looking specifically at men or women, children or Elders, as the chapter titles would indicate. Rather, we are coming to know the flows of energy—sexual energy and time energy—of which these age and gender groups are a part. We are complex beings, comprised of a blend of male-female and child-Elder energies. In each of us, the blend is unique, making us perhaps more female than male, or more child than Elder; the varying degrees of these energies being intrinsic to our makeup.

Recognizing, understanding, and developing each of these energies within us is what fuels our Journey, because they control the basic motivations of our life—growth and reproduction. So in the coming pages as we step further into the lives of Old Way People, let us keep in mind that we are not viewing roles or lifeways specific to any gender or age—we are looking at the flow of energies that is you and that is me.

The balance of sexual energies within us is a good illustration of that flow. When we attune ourselves to these energies, we discover that we are a blend of male and female; we each have the hormones of both sexes flowing in our blood. So we are not a particular sex in an absolute sense, but in manner of degree. Both sexes share the same chemistry and urgings; the difference lies only in degree and intensity. In a clinical sense, we are all bisexual.

This Old Way understanding of each of us being the expression of an energy continuum does not mesh well with Civilization's penchant for pigeon-holing its members into neat black-and-white categories based on physical characteristics or sexual preference. For instance, I, who am labelled a male, have the same hormones as a female. In fact, there may be less difference in hormonal balance between a particular female and me than between another male and me.

The following chart illustrates this continuum. The paired vertical bars (white-centered are female, black-centered are male) represent the various possible levels of male and female energies in each of us. Each pair is labelled with the physical, sexual expression it manifests. Immediately below that chart is another, showing the relative numbers of people in each pairing.

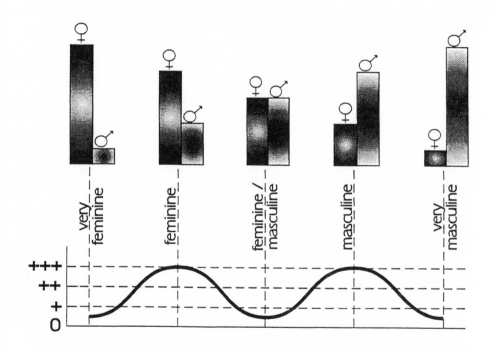

Charts 8 & 9. Male-Female Energy Combinations (above)
and Numbers of People in Each Combination (below)

The first pairing, which is very high in female energy and very low in male energy, represents people with strongly developed feminine physical and behavioral characteristics and very little expression of the male within them. There are relatively few of these women. The second pairing represents most women—strong female energy in conjunction with a smaller, though visible, component of male energy.

The center pairing, in which both energies are roughly equal, includes a seemingly wide diversity of people— physical females who are behaviorally male, physical males who are behaviorally female, and those who exhibit some of the physical characteristics of both sexes. These include women with strong masculine behavioral characteristics, men who are very expressively effeminate, and hermaphrodites (physiologically both male and female). When we step back from the categorizing, we see that these people are actually quite similar to one another in the intrinsic expression of their sexuality. They form the continuum in the flow between the energies of each sex.

In Old Way cultures these people are often honored and serve important functions. They are considered total people, having the power and energy of both sexes and being bound by the limitations of neither. Because of this gift, they become the Healers and Spirit-talkers.

As in the second pairing for women, most men are represented in the fourth pairing—dominant male energy with a viable female complement. And as the first pairing depicts the ultra-female, the last one shows the ultra-male, whose strongly masculine side leaves little space for the expression of its greatly diminished female counterpart.

If Civilized People would begin to view each other first as individuals, each with a unique sexuality that is not clearly or exclusively male or female, perhaps much of the pain and misunderstanding that now exists between the sexes would fade.

Our sexuality is something to be proud of and revel in, as it is the vehicle that carries our personal gifts to our People. Our creativity, our heart, our sweat would have no fire without it. Living in the fullness and richness of our sexuality is giving honor to self and praise to Creation; not doing so is denying self and Creation.

Love and Mating

In our Hoop of Life, our sexuality is most fully expressed with our mate. We use the term "love" to express this special sharing. In the Civilized Way, love is seen as being rooted within each person, whereas in the Old Way, it is viewed as a sharing in something that exists beyond the self. The

Civilized perception causes mates to look at each other and say they are "living for each other;" in the Old Way lovers look in the same direction toward the Greater Life.

The love of Civilized People drew inward when they seceded from the Earth culture and thereby lost touch with the Universal Love. The honored traditions of its ancient wisdoms and functional practicality went with it, and the new bonding force, which we'll call "romantic love," found its roots only in mind and emotion.

Not having the perspective of Old Way love, Civilized People are prone to look at the pairing of some Native Peoples as being arranged—decided by someone other than the involved couple. This practice may seem to be an insensitive and archaic means of coupling, as people seem to be thrown together without regard for their own feelings and desires.

This is often the case in cultures that are on the interface between their Old Ways and encroaching Civilization. Economics becomes a consideration in mate selection, and Native wisdoms lose their power and relevance to the omnipresent conflicts of new ways. Customs and rituals become hollow vestiges of their past, buoyed and perpetuated by dogmatic zeal and rote standardization newly acquired from their Civilized neighbors.

However, arranged marriages in the Old Way are stable, long-lived, productive, and steeped in love. The arranged part is sometimes just an affirmation of that which is obviously intended to be. Those that can more truly be considered to be arranged involve values and perspectives that someone outside the culture may not be aware of or capable of grasping.

One very important consideration is that mates are chosen by those of wisdom who know not only the individuals, but their parents, relatives, Ancestors, and Clan. In some ways they know the individuals better than the individuals know themselves. They see their past and they see their future. These insights give them far greater success at selecting mates than does the flush of romantic love.

A romantic marriage begins with love; an arranged marriage grows into love. In lieu of this romantic force, an arranged marriage draws its initial power from strength of culture and the love and nurturance it shares with its People.

Civilized marriages usually flounder in their first years, because they do not have the strength of this support. Many of those that survive are cruel attempts at maintaining togetherness. There is little substance, as they are strangers to each other—they lack communion of spirit and Vision. They form isolated nuclear families, attempting to survive without the guidance of Elders and the support of relations. When they part, single parent families are born, further diluting the already slight and fragile support base.

In the Old Way, mates can literally be each others' mirrors; they help to groom and dress one another. This indicates a necessary level of trust and esteem (self and mutual), which is common to the Old Way. With this awareness in mind, let us continue meeting People of the Old Way.

Elders
Jean Briggs, *Never in Anger: Portrait of an Eskimo Family*
Robert Dentian, *The Semai: A Nonviolent People of Malaya*
Edward Dozier, *Hano: a Tewa Indian Community in Arizona*
Daniel J. Levinson, *A Conception of Adult Development*
    (In Jan.'86 *American Psychologist), The Seasons of a Man's Life*
Jean Liedloff, *The Continuum Concept*
Elsie Clews Parsons, *American Indian Life*
Colin Turnbull, *The Forest People: A Study of the Pygmies of the Congo*

Pigeon is held sacred in the ancient cultures . . .
Through the spirit of Pigeon I have traveled within the spirit of all birds.

The reign of the Mother Moon is a flamboyant, high-energy time,
conducive to birthing, releasing, reaching out, and sharing.

Sisters of the Moon

Moon's pale light reflected off of the Hoopdrums like a circle of Fireflies flashing to the rhythm of the shrill chant. Virtually every woman came to the High Meadow that night, called into ritual by the pregnant fullness of their Moon Sister.

Earlier in the day, the camp was in conflict. The talk of revenge went on into the night, growing more heated with the fuel of alcohol and unleashed repression. The women protested but went unheard. For too many generations, they took it upon themselves to soothe the rage and absorb the pain.

Late that night, like a Wind crying in the high Pines, the throbbing wail of the women drifted down the quiet hillside to the camp below. The intense, eerie sound penetrated the Lodges, bringing the men to sober attention. The younger ones could not remember ever having heard such a sound, and the older ones grew quiet and introspective.

Without a word, the older men began drifting, one by one, back to their family Lodges. The remaining men eventually followed. When the women came down from the clearing, they found their men asleep, and after that night heard no more of revenge.

An Elder Medicine woman recounted to me this memory from her childhood. She was told by her Grandmother to stay behind and go back to sleep, but she secretly followed the women up to the clearing anyway and observed their ritual.

Our Journey now brings us to a vital step in our healing, and perhaps also to a glimpse of the transformative wisdom the Civilized Way needs in order to entertain thoughts of a future. On this step, let us bear in mind that much of what we meet is not just about and for women, but for the womanness in each of us, regardless of gender and age. As a man who honors and encourages the womanness in himself, and as a person who was touched by the sensitivities and has sought the guidance of Old Way Women, I respectfully (and sometimes awkwardly) talk with you of Womanpower.

Honor Her Culture

The Native woman is confident of her role in her society, as she is an integral, contributing member, possessed of the skills and self-fulfillment that give her identity and autonomy. She is wrapped in the embrace of her People. If she were widowed or if she or her children were orphaned, she is secure in the knowledge that her band would provide shelter and care.

She works in partnership with men, in a complementary, nurturing way. The affairs of subsistence are divided between the sexes, usually along the lines of what is most appropriate to the ability of each sex. Because the contributions of both are necessary, they are both valued. So the rank, freedom, and power of men and women over their lives are more likely to be on a par than in the Civilized cultures, where sex roles are commonly based more on conventional divisions of labor than ability or interest.

In many Old Way cultures, sex roles are loosely defined and are not based entirely on gender. The lighter work of men may be assisted by women, and the more strenuous labors of women may be aided by men. In these societies, women are free to pursue traditional men's roles, and the woman in man is respected and given room for expression. Both are openly accepted but fully expected to perform on a par with their peers. And there are broad areas of overlap where both sexes work together on tasks that are appropriate to either or that require the skills of both.

In this day of growing feminist consciousness in the Civilized societies, there is a tendency amongst non-Natives to view the roles of Native women in their societies from a dogmatic feminist perspective. In doing so, Native women—and all the Civilized women and men involved in the hard walk through sexually-based oppression—are being done a great disservice.

The Civilized world is so dissimilar from the world of the Native woman that her role in it can be clearly and fairly understood only by viewing it within the context of her culture. However, the unfortunate tendency of the Civilized is to view the divisions of labor and "primitive" technologies of her lifeway as backward and demeaning. An immersed perspective— taking on her eyes and heart—would carry Power and valuable wisdoms to the feminist movement.

There is a Civilized bias that favors societal over family involvements. Political and economic activities are viewed with esteem, while those that are oriented around nurturing and crafts are considered commonplace. This bias gives men the illusion of freedom and fulfillment and leaves women with feelings of restriction and subjugation.

Imagine if the stereotypical female skills were valued and standard male involvements were considered mundane. Then perhaps men would feel maligned and consider women to be privileged and oppressive. Even though the cultural context and societal rules remain the same, the perceptual difference alone turns the status of both genders topsy-turvy. So imagine what could (and does) happen when one culture's perceptual perspective is applied to another culture with a different approach to sexuality, divisions of labor, and living values . . .

This being the situation, there are often strong cultural biases levied particularly against the Old Way customs associated with women's Moontime (menses). Both cultural anthropologists and lay people consider some of these practices, particularly the isolation of women in Moontime, to be male taboos enforced against women. They perceive the men as segregating the women because they are unclean. From the perspective of the people involved, these accomodations are just a recognition of, and a living in Balance with, natural cycles and energies. The rest of this chapter is a look at how these sisters of the Moon walk with themselves and their People in their Moontime.

Moontime Power and Spirit

Native women honor the Moon and follow Her ceremonial ways. Regularly bathed in Her light, their Mooncycles are drawn into ritual sync with Hers. Mother Moon (Full Moon) is their Fertile Time, and Dead (New) Moon is their time of bleeding (or Moontime). Women who are in their Moontime during New Moon generally have an easy time of it. (Because of their good physical condition, Old Way women in general have little pain or discomfort. A hard Moontime can be a sign of poor condition or some other imbalance.)

The intensity of Moontime and Fertiletime and the degree of personal involvement naturally varies from woman to woman. The reign of Mother Moon is a flamboyant, high-energy time, conducive to birthing, releasing, reaching out, and sharing. Women are at the height of their male Power. New Moon draws women into themselves, bringing on a creatively active, introspective time, a returning to the Womb (akin to the Sweat Lodge Ceremony and a reason women infrequently enter the Sweat Lodge). As Moon is in Her dying, women gradually become quieter and more withdrawn. They may seem sensitive to irritation by those near them who are not also entering Moontime.

They are entering a period of intense Personal Power—instinctive/intuitive energies are high, sensory and physical abilities are low, and emotions are set free to ride and empower. Inspirations abound, as do Blessings of reflective and introspective clarity. This time is the budding; in the Mother Moon is the flowering.

At this time, the Veil is naturally raised between the first and second awarenesses (covered in Sensory Attunement chapter), and women are most centered in their Heart-of-Hearts. They are well-attuned to the Voices and can make dramatic progress on their Paths. Their Dreamtime pathway is also easily traveled; powerful Prophetic and Manifesting Dreams can be given. Many women receive their Dreampaths (Visions) during Moontime (and so do not need to Quest for Vision as often as do men).

The Gifts that come in the Dreams and Voices are intended for the People. As Dead Moon gives, so Pregnant Moon is for giving. It is the time for women, as nurturers, to walk beyond themselves as their Peoples' Prophets and Healers.

In the bleeding is the Power of healing. In the Moontime blood is the source of life renewed, so it is from there that the Healer draws to regenerate herself or to effect the healing of others. Male Healers also come to this source (either as it abides in them or as it is provided by women) for their Healing Power.

Besides having the Power of healing, women are natural Healers because of the birthing experience. In order to become a Healer one must first face her own death without fear and then re-enter life. In doing so, she gains the necessary intimate knowledge of the cycle of life-energy. In giving birth, women greet the prospect of their own passing-over with courage, not knowing if she will return after her gifting of life for the continuance of her People.

The Healer gives without expectation of return, doing so by stepping out of herself and entering the state of second awareness, then giving herself to the healing. This is what women do in childbirth. (At the loss of their healing Gift for their People, many Civilized women do not have this empowering experience because they are denied a natural childbirth. In an unfamiliar, sterile environment, often without the touch of women Healers, they are deprived of their threshold experience to becoming Healers by mechanical or chemical intercession.)

For accomplished women of Medicine, New Moon is the time of Roaring Power. New Moon infuses their innate Powers with a lush potency that gives their healings greater effectiveness. This energy is drawn from sources especially petitioned by the women to lend power to their specific Medicine.

A woman Healer who is beyond Moontime may ask a younger woman who is in her Moontime, and with whom she is spiritually compatible, to lend her Moontime Power to help effect a healing. This young woman is often an apprentice to the Healer and will remain an apprentice for many, many years—perhaps until she herself walks beyond Moontime. This time of training and ascetic discipline is the common Path to becoming a woman of Medicine. It is walked with a depth of dedication and perseverance that carries her through to the completion of her apprenticeship. (The duration and degree of her commitment is a powerful example of clarity of Vision and sense of dedication to one's People.)

Some women practice Medicine only in their Moontimes because it is their time of Power and because it is an unfettered, quiet time. (They tend to their craft more regularly after their children have grown and they have walked beyond Moontime.) It is possible but rare for a younger Healer to practice her craft when not in her Moontime. The ability to gain focus on her Moon energies and summon and use them at any time takes many years, if ever, to acomplish before walking beyond Moontime.

An Herbalist would probably not risk gathering, preparing, or blending herbs when in her Moontime, because of the powerful and possibly contradictory energies at play.

Most women are not able to handle the wonderous but potentially volatile mix that is Moontime within the context of their normal daily lives. They need the time and space to honor these energies and walk with them.

The Civilized approach is to suppress these "symptoms" of the "necessary evil" of womanhood and have them contend with life as usual. The personal cost to women is what is contemporarily labeled as Pre-Menstrual Syndrome—a catch-all label for the distorted moods and behaviors resulting from suppression. The prescribed cure is often behavior-modification through drugs and therapy to simulate "normalcy."

Those who do not allow women to Honor their Moontime pay a high cost—the depriving of themselves and their People of womens' special Gifts. They go undiscovered, undeveloped, ungifted. The culture becomes imbalanced, its ways contorted and blinded from the loss of womens' contribution. Based on the track record of other cultures whose People have dishonored Moontime, the final cost is likely their culture's eventual demise.

No matter what the denial or psycho-emotional adjustment, women cannot do everything that men can do and still honor the sacred time of their womanhood. Many view the full functioning of women in male-created and dominated roles as liberating, whereas such mimicry may actually be giving tacit approval and empowerment to the suppression of woman-expression.

In the Old Way, women are expected to act, think, and speak differently than men. Women in their Moontimes are allowed and encouraged their "unordinary" behavior. They often have a special place to go, a place where they can leave their physical routine behind, step aside from their emotional involvements, and give free reign to their intensified energies. This is in balance with their natural inclinations at this time, which tend toward self-absorption and reclusiveness (one reason being their increased sensitivity to Sun).

A special Moonlodge may be set up behind her family lodge, where she spends the several days that she is in her Moontime. With other People, it is the custom to set up a large lodge or a cluster of individual lodges a short distance from their village, where the women spend their Moontimes together. (Women in close proximity to each other become senitive to, and influence, each other's rhythms. This, along with Moon's influence, draws their Mooncycles into sync, bringing them together in the Moonlodge.)

A quiet, secluded place is usually chosen for the Lodge. The atmosphere around the Lodge is important because of women's heightened sensitivity and receptivity, and because what is absorbed in Moontime will emanate in Fertiletime.

On occasion, women will use their Moonlodge for similar purpose when they are not in their Moontimes. Although not a common practice, men may also have a special lodge where they can go to spend alone time.

In some respects, the Moonlodge is for women what the Sweat Lodge is for men. Women are usually in their Moonlodge on the Dead Moon, which is the time She most strongly draws Womanpower; men regularly enter the Sweat Lodge on the Pregnant Moon, as She then empowers maleness.

Women who have walked beyond their Moontimes, being little affected by the energy of the Moonlodge, often tend to their sisters therein. They bring fresh absorbent materials, such as cattail down or moss, and take the used materials to dispose of in a sacred manner, as the blood has a power and a life of its own. Some women gift their blood directly to The Mother or use it in ritual healing.

Smaller and more nomadic groups such as Desert People or People of the Far North may not have Moonlodges. And a woman might not go to the Moonlodge when there is not a woman past Moontime to tend her household. In these cases, adjustments are made within the context of family and lodge so that her Moontime is honored and her needs are met. The rest of the family will do her tasks, and they will remove their personal Medicine objects so that they do not interfere with her energy.

Women regularly fast during their Moontimes to aid in their spiritual attunement. In some cultures, the fast is a partial one, with Desert People perhaps abstaining from water or other People refraining from a specific mainstay food. Sometimes ceremonies are conducted in the Moonlodge, also for the purpose of spiritual attunement.

One Lodge Ceremony is that of First Blood—the Rite of Transition that accepts a girl into womanhood. She is honored for successfully coming to Passage and is instructed in the ways and skills of a woman for which she was previously too young. At this time she may begin dressing and adorning herself differently to indicate that she is now a woman.

When leaving the Moonlodge, women may partake in a ritual bathing. This is done downstream from other human activities, partly to preserve the special and separate aspect of this last act of their Mooncycle, and partly so that they don't affect others with their energy.

Native People know that the highly spiritualized state of women in their Moontimes is a gift that carries with it the responsibility to use its powers conscientiously. Not to do so carries the risk of diffusing or scrambling the energy of others who must rely upon the integrity of their power for success in their tasks. Healers who rely on other than Moontime energies are particularly vulnerable, but those of other crafts and skills may also be affected.

The Hunter, for instance, needs to reach a quality of spiritual Balance that will allow him to speak with the animal intended for him and ask for the gift of her body. Along with bringing meat to his People, his task involves providing an abiding place within himself for the animal's spirit. Together with her flesh, her spirit will become a part of each of those who partake.

Quest for Balance

Women who are of the People seldom Quest for Vision or partake in the Sweat Lodge Ceremony. Along with the reason already mentioned, women are more naturally attuned to spiritual and Earth energies than men, so they don't have to strive for Balance as strongly as men do (see Mental Attunement chapter). Women who are called to the Medicine Way may Vision Quest, and women Warriors and Hunters partake in the purification rite of the Sweat Lodge, as they have the need to cleanse and attune themselves to the common mission, just as do men.

Some Elders are now saying that in this time of healing, it is good and desirable for women—all women who are opening to the Voices of Earth and Ancients—to Cry for Vision and to enter the Sweat Lodge. They ask women to do this both with their sisters, and with their estranged brothers who share the struggle.

A Lakota Elder whom I recently met says that male and female twins share the same womb, so it is natural for women and men to share the Sweat Lodge. (The Sweat Lodge is the Womb of The Mother, and leaving it is being reborn.)

Women (and men) caught in the Civilized Way have been denied access to their own natural skills and innate senses; they now need to work—independently and with their mates and People—to regain their Power and realign themselves with Earth and Moon rhythms.

Elders
Grand Marais, MN School District, *The Anishinabe Woman*
Anne Cameron, *Daughters of Copper Woman*
Ruth Landes, *The Ojibwa Woman*
Yolanda and Robert Murphy, *Women of the Forest*
Vicki Noble, *Female Blood: Roots of Shamanism* (from Spring '86 *Shaman's Drum*)
Spider, *Songs of Bleeding*

Native women honor the Moon and follow Her ceremonial ways.

. . . she slowly began transforming into Raven —
black feathers glistening in the firelight, black eyes echoing the dance of the sparks.

The Way of the Warrior

One evening when the Campfire sparks were jumping high into the blackness, I asked She Who Talks With Loons why there are so few Warriors amongst Civilized People. As usual, I got no answer—at least not one I would recognize as such. Then as I raised my head to look at her across the Fire, she slowly began transforming into Raven—black feathers glistening in the firelight, black eyes echoing the dance of the sparks. Her eye caught mine, and we spoke in the voiceless language I was slowly growing accustomed to.

In reply to my question, she said (in a way to be sure I took her as stating the obvious), "Because the Path of the Warrior no longer exists for them." Once again, I felt stupid for not being able to see the obvious for myself. Yet I was grateful for her shaming me into seeing what I couldn't see before. I didn't even mind the glint in her eye, which told me she was delighted by the process.

We talked on in the company of the dying embers. She played the Inquisitor, helping me to grasp how much I already knew: the remaining Warriors of the Civilized Way had been jailed or executed or banished long, long ago, and any memory of their existence lives on only in legends and fairytales. In these lands where the only sanctioned voices are those of the priest and the politician and the moneychanger, there is no place for those who hear the Mother's Voice. These entrenched rulers fancy their power being threatened by the existence of an allegiance within a realm outside their control.

She told me of those she knew who were being called to be Warriors but didn't know the Voice to recognize it. They were out of step with the realm of their existence. They couldn't find a niche for themselves, couldn't find fulfillment, and they didn't know why. They were not happy People. A Warrior, or one whose destiny is to be one, is not an adaptable person and doesn't have the option of choosing another Path.

By the sadness in her ember-tinted eyes, I could tell she had nothing to say to them, nothing to offer. I felt it was partly because there was no way she could touch their pain with words. To such a hollow pain, words are as appropriate as snowshoes are to a Turtle. And it was partly because the form of their culture was so different from hers; there was no ready bridge.

They weren't given the time or wherewithal to walk together with the Ancestors and seep themselves in those Old Ways that would give them the oneness of heart to touch on such things. And realistically, there was nothing she alone could offer, there was no place to send them to be guided on their given Path. I sensed her feelings of impotence; I know that a little bit of her died each time a lost, unknowing Warrior walked away from her, because she knew what he was walking into.

Bold and ruthless, male, leading a colorful life of glory and adventure, always ready for battle—this is the stereotypical Warrior to the Civilized People. And not surprisingly. They met him as the cutting edge of the worldwide Native resistance to their endless march. His People, his Mother, and his lifeway were under seige; he was in constant preparedness for war. They knew him only as a fighter because genocide was their only diplomacy.

The stereotype is perpetuated in the Civilized Peoples' romanticized recountings of their conquests, fueled by their fixation on violence and cultural chauvinism. This chapter is not about that Warrior. But before we meet and walk with the real Warrior of The People, let us honor him with proper title.

Warrior as Guardian

> warrior: 1. a man engaged or experienced in warfare and espe-
> cially in primitive warfare or the close combat of ancient or
> medieval times. 2. a person of demonstrated courage, forti-
> tude, zeal, or pugnacity.
> —Webster's Third New International Dictionary

The term "warrior" is derived from an Old Germanic word, which Civilized usage has corrupted to the point that, at present, it is known primarily by the first definition above. It retains some of its original meaning in the second definition. However, the first definition is so entrenched and all-pervasive that using the term would further perpetuate the stereotype, and trying to return it to its original definition would, like so many other struggles with the Civilized Way, be energy better spent elsewhere.

Instead, we will use "Guardian," a parallel Old French word that by some sparing miracle has not met the same fate as "Warrior." The same dictionary cited above gives its definitions as: one that guards or secures: one to whom a person or thing is committed for protection, security, or preservation. This was also the meaning of the term "Warrior" as it was used in the Old Way.

We are meeting the Guardian in our quest to know the men (as well as some women and the man within woman) of the Old Way because he exemplifies the role of maleness in Native cultures. The Guardian tradition is common to virtually all Old Way Peoples. He is a highly defined individual, many of whose characteristics are those of Native males in general. He is also an element of the Native psyche; he dwells in all the People, regardless of age or gender. (For Balance, many Native People purposely cultivate the expression of their less dominant gender.)

There are some who feel that there is no place for the Guardian in this Civilized day. In one sense this is true, as the man's lifestyle (more so than the woman's) has been severely disrupted in the transition from the Old to the Civilized Way. No longer are the Hunter and the Guardian viable parts of the family support system, whereas the woman's caretaking roles with children and hearth, albeit changed, still are. Men have trouble maintaining a sense of self-worth in such circumstances, much less functioning as Guardians.

In another sense, The Great Mother now calls upon Her Guardians with an urgent battle cry, the likes of which have never before echoed through the realms of Her Creation. The People of Greenpeace and Earth First!, single mothers, Natives who keep the Drum and refuse the spirit-death—all these people, and more, are answering the cry. They embody the Vision of the Guardian and have joined in the struggle to return to Balance.

We're all Guardians. Whenever we act on our Mother's or our kin's calling, our Ancestors who were once Guardians walk again on their Vision Path. Whether or not we were called to walk that Path, they give us breath, and we give them life. They are the reason for the survival of our lineage—the reason we are here.

The Calling

The Path of the Guardian is one that we do not choose, but for which we are chosen. It is a most honorable calling to serve; it is being ordained to take one's place as a caretaker of The Mother and Her children. When the Path is understood and the Old Ways of our Ancestors are reawakened within our Heart-of-Hearts, we will know clearly whether The Great Mother has called us to Her service.

The Way of the Guardian takes a level of dedication, commitment, and Vision that an individual can't muster alone. It takes melding with the Greater Life, the Ultimate Wisdom. No one would decide on this Path to further his own ends. From a personal perspective it wouldn't make sense, because it demands so much of the self that it would contradict personal goal fulfillment.

But it is the only thing to do, the most fulfilling and rewarding life for one who hears the Cry. It is so clear that if he does not answer it, he lives a life of flatness and despondency. He is out of sync with the rhythm of his Heart-of-Hearts; he cannot get a grasp on that inner Balance that brings blessings to life.

The Way of the Guardian is the epitome of a life lived in Balance, because it is the giving of the greatest gift—the gift of self. His Path is rooted strongly in his Hoop of Relations, as it is there that his life of service begins. It is the strength of his Hoop that gives power to his Path. As he leaves his Hoop, he becomes part of a greater organism that is made up of many Hoops. He is a vital web in the net that holds the Hoops together. As a Guardian, he has no life, no purpose, when separated from that organism. He is like a finger, which has function and reason for being only when part of the hand.

To a civilian, the Guardian's life may appear to be one of deprivation and Spartan discipline. To the Guardian it is a life of bliss, the only Path there is. It is being immersed in another consciousness, existing in another reality.

The Apprenticeship

Life is a gift; we honor The Great Mother who gave it to us by giving it, in turn, to that which honors Her. Such is the ritualistic offering of self of one who enters the training period to become a Guardian. In actuality, the preparation begins long before the formal Apprenticeship; all Native children are schooled in the skills of the lifeway. The Guardian Apprenticeship involves specialized training in a broad range of disciplines that carry the Apprentice far beyond the average performance range of his peers. He may be adopted by a revered and accomplished Guardian of his People, who will oversee his training. He will also study under a number of other practitioners to gain breadth and depth of abilities.

The Apprenticeship is a series of experiences and tests. It is a long, demanding, and glorious adventure, which asks for nothing less than his life as he knows it. He enters a period in which he is transformed; he receives new Powers, enlivened senses, and the ability to act as though his spirit is the spirit of his People. In surrendering to the task of training, he erases the limits he once had of himself and enters a realm of unbounded creativity and expression.

Serving a Guardian Apprenticeship requires the same level of dedication and involvement as joining a monastic order; the difference is that, in the Guardian Apprenticeship, there is no hierarchical structure or imposed regimentation. Discipline and motivation come from within. In effect, he apprentices to himself. He has a Guide, who reflects and facilitates and echoes Raven's occasional subtle nudge and inquisitive eye.

The Apprentice has an unswerving commitment to his Guide. The commitment is actually to The Great Mother and the Ancient Voices, which the Guide personifies until the Guardian himself becomes the personification.

To assist a Guardian Apprentice in his training is one of a Guides' greatest honors. The relationship between Apprentice and Guide is a very special one—in fact, unique in the spectrum of Guide-Seeker relationships. It is in answer to a calling similar to that which draws a mother to her far-off child. They share a clarity, discipline, and degree of attunement that makes their time together a Dance.

These are the steps of the Path to becoming a Guardian:

— to become fully alive, fully aware,

— to develop talents, senses, instincts, intuitions,

— to release habits and patterns,

— to become self by becoming selfless,

— to be ever aware that life as a Guardian is a continuing Journey, that there will always be another step, but not before the last one is fully taken,

— to accept protectorship of the People, caretakership of The Mother, and stewardship of self, and

— to perform one grand feat in the service of his Guide. (This is both a final test and a return gifting for what has been given.)

Many of the techniques and exercises involved in these steps are found in the next two parts of this volume, and in Book II.

During his Apprenticeship, his behavior may at times become erratic and unpredictable. He finds himself struggling with new Powers and energies, trying to mesh them with his newly evolving concept of self. Contraries and images from his past regularly test him. What he perceived as his limits have been pushed out beyond what he could previously envision.

His Guide allows and often encourages this erratic behavior, as he knows it is part of the growth and transformation process. However, his Guide faces a tremendous challenge in bringing him to a state of equilibrium as he nears the end of his Apprenticeship. The Guide must be a master at reading the intricacies and complexities of an individual's psyche in order to direct the appropriate experiences at this critical time.

Respect

Respect describes the Guardian and all he is and does—respect of Earth and all She encompasses and respect of self. He is a highly attuned spiritual/physical being, entrusted with the welfare of his People. In this role he plays many roles—provider, defender, arbitrator, counsellor, healer, and, at times, opportunist and predator. He is dedicated to self-improvement, so that he can become ever better at making Respect his Lifedance.

The mark of a Guardian is in the way he continually encourages himself to grow by taking the (or creating a) more challenging alternative, and by teasing the edge of seeming disaster. (This is the reverse of the Civilized Way, which is one reason why its unknowing Guardian-elects are caught in leading—or attempting to escape—flat, uninspired lives.)

In the first pages of this book, I recount how She Who Talks With Loons brought me the Gift of Being Nothing—the ability to step beyond oneself and let other things flow through. It is an essential step in becoming a Guardian. To become aware that he is not his ego, that what dwells beyond him is not as he perceives it, brings him a humility and an openness that allows him to begin listening for the first time. Then he can start using channels previously plugged by pride and youthful haughtiness. Shame and embarrassment leave him, as they are based on ego-bolstered pride. He becomes able to grow into a self-pride and a self-honor that is independent of ego and the opinions of others.

We develop an ego, in part, as a defense mechanism to protect the self from others who have a concept of us that differs from ours. We hold the ego as a shield to buffer us from what we consider to be personal affronts. We perceive them as such mainly because of low self-acceptance and lack of Circle Attunement. Our shield is feelings such as hurt, shame, pride, and embarrassment. These feelings rigidify and entrench us in emotional stagnation, which impedes our ability to dwell in the now of our Circle and be responsive to it.

The Guardian has died to his ego and walked beyond it. (Some of his techniques for doing so are found in Part IV of this volume and in the Healing chapter of Book III.) He has a strong sense of self and manner of presence; he can speak of his quests and deeds without self-consciousness and self-imposed humility. And he can listen to the stories of another without ego-ripping pangs of vanity and jealousy. In fact, he and his comrades glory in each others' triumphs and in sharing the pain of each others' defeats.

From React to Act

The Guardian does not fight against anything or anyone; he fights *for* things. When he meets conflict on his mission, his high degree of training in methods of camouflage, avoidance, and deception allows him to cause the least impact upon others and their Paths. He has a highly attuned spiritual sense for the Life-force in others as being the same as that which flows through him, so he accords those who stand in his Path utmost respect and space.

If there is no other way, he is also highly trained to remove them in the most efficient, least harmful way possible. In this respect, the Guardian is often cast as "cool and efficient," and "heartless." Such is not his reality. He may *appear* detached, which is only because he never acts out of anger, lust, or grief and never strikes in a state of rage.

When and if he finds himself in such a state, he backs off rather than striking. He knows he is out of Balance and has temporarily lost his critical sense of perspective and attunement. He does not serve when he responds from a personal place. Besides being blinded to all but his own spirit-flow, his emotions have taken control and narrowed his eyes, making him extremely vulnerable.

This is not to say that the Guardian's actions are not imbued with feeling. On the contrary, this training serves to heighten the power of emotion. A distinguishing characteristic of a Guardian is that his changes in mood and temperament come from within. They are deliberate, controlled, and purposeful. And they are timely—they are enacted and drawn upon to give power to his service. In other words, his feelings serve rather than master him.

He exhibits a calmness and stability that is little affected by the happenings about him. He is trained to function from his center (also known as his Place of Power or Heart-of-Hearts). This gives Balance to his perspective and continuity to his actions. And it gives his People trust in his Guardianship, because they know the source and motivation of his actions.

He trains to allow his feelings to be those of the Greater Circle, seeing himself as but a part of that larger Life that gives him breath and purpose. As his hand feels and acts for the benefit of his entire body, so does he function in relation to the Greater Circle. Being of the Old Way, he already knows that honoring the Circle is the best way to honor himself; now, as a Guardian Apprentice, he learns that it is also the best way to honor his People.

In training, he consciously maintains this awareness of being as a hand to a body. When a personally based response to a situation surfaces, he shuts down and disassociates himself from the situation, so as not to reinforce the personal response pattern. Then he enters a state of Greater Circle consciousness and reapproaches the situation.

Just as near-sighted Mouse cannot see the Prairie from the perspective of soaring Eagle, the Apprentice cannot at first differentiate between the response that comes from himself and that which comes from the consciousness level of the Circle. His Guide must be ever vigilant in training to constantly catch his personal responses and help realign his response patterns to be sensitive to that which he serves.

Without this training, he would be of little service to his People. His actions would actually be *re*-actions—emotional responses based upon his personal feelings in relation to similar past experiences. Reactions, being personal, patterned, and habitual, dictate rigid behavior and predictability. This would leave the Guardian vulnerable to his enemies and inflexible in responding to the needs of his People.

One method of training identifies feelings that come from past patterns of service to self as *old emotions*, and those which come from discipline in service to the Circle as *new emotions*. Before training, the Apprentice served to empower old emotions; after training, new emotions will serve to empower him.

He learns that old emotions are based upon *his* perspective on how past events affected *him*. His Guide aids him in reliving those events from the Greater Perspective. Through this process, he begins to feel new emotions when an event occurs. Every new experience then helps to establish new emotion reaction patterns (see Healing chapter in Book III).

The process from old to new emotions can be long and painful. Being a creature of habit, the Apprentice trusts in his habitual responses. To rock that foundation is to rock his concept of self, his value as an individual. For that reason, this aspect of training, perhaps more than any other, requires trust in his Guide and surety in the fact that his Guide's actions serve the Greater Good. This is one of the situations in which he will be asked to fight to the top of the hill, with little awareness as to what he will view when he peers over the summit.

A different person, a new person, will be seen by others when he does clear the summit. His image to others is based upon his reactions to his environment; so, reacting differently, he will evolve a new identity. However, from his perspective inward, he is not a new person—he has just completed a step in his Journey of self-discovery. He, having grown through his old ego-center, now senses from the same center as the Wolves and the Wind.

His old reactive pattern was to feel first, then act upon the feeling, then think about the situation based upon his feeling and the result of his action. Oftentimes he would cloak his feeling in rationalizations to justify his action. From his new center, his second awareness listens to his intuitive voice and then elicits feeling and thought to support his action. (In the next part of this book, we begin the training.)

Now, no matter where he is or what his involvement, the Guardian can maintain his new identity and sense of self, because they are not dependent on his internal or external environments. Even when regularly around other people, he has no particular need for alone time. He rarely gets tripped up on other individuals, nor does he get carried away by them.

A Guardian owns nothing. The vested interest of ownership could color his perception and distort his judgement. Just as his energy, spirit, and emotions are for the service of his People and under the guidance of the Greater Circle, so are the worldly goods that come under his care. He will share often with one in need, to his own apparent discomfort or deprivation.

If a Guardian ever senses that his actions may be in the service of something that is not in honor of the Greater Good, he will desist and withdraw in shame. He may return to his Guide and petition for assistance so that he can regain faith in himself and the trust of his People—and most importantly—in the eyes of The Mother. If he commits a grave breach of trust, he may relinquish his service and return to civilian life.

A Guardian need not be asked to leave his service, as he is aware of his failing and has taken immediate, appropriate action. This is in line with his training, as it is in his honor to know himself and act accordingly for the Greater Good. It is dishonorable and self-aggrandizing to attempt to remain a Guardian in the face of disservice. When a Guardian returns to normal life, he maintains the respect and esteem of his People. Because they have a limited understanding of the Guardian's world, and they respect his choice to leave, they give honor to his former service by not prying into his reasons. The Guardian maintains self-esteem as well, because in relinquishing his service he is serving his People.

Leaving Habit, Living Awareness

The vow of renunciation of worldly goods and pleasures taken by Civilized People (when entering a religious order or other service) is a rote, institutionalized relic of the threshold experience of the Apprentice's Quest to walk beyond himself. The act of renunciation, while seeming to maintain the essence of the Quest, actually contradicts it. The Guardian walks beyond himself by embracing, rather than renouncing, the physical realm. He metamorphoses into his ascetic, serving self through the wisdom of knowing; his Civilized brother arrives by force of denial, and in doing so, denies knowing himself.

Self-control necessitates some form of self-repression, which usually creates enough stress to clog the senses and interfere with the lifting of the Veil to the second awareness (see Sensory Attunement chapter). Eliminating renunciation and self-control as an option opens one up to the challenge and opportunity to grow into acceptance. For example: If Porcupine chews up my canoe paddle in the night because she is attracted to the salt from my sweat, I can react with resignation, with anger (and either repress, rechannel, or revent it), or by thanking Porcupine for the lesson in appropriate paddle storage and welcoming the opportunity to improve my paddlemaking skills.

The Guardian comes to self-discipline through self-indulgence. In an explosion of total attunement and involvement, he drinks in life to its fullest. Being in the now, being the embodiment of his Ancestors, and fulfilling his innate potential, he is content within himself and in Balance with the Circles of his existence. He is in charge of himself. Sacrifice and deprivation are as easy as laxity and indulgence, because they as equally and powerfully Dance in celebration of life in the present. They're just as easy because the Guardian sees them this way. Everything, every experience, is a feast, a Song of the moment, an affirmation of self.

He can just as easily pass over food as indulge, just as easily fight as dance, just as easily give as receive, because he is secure, fulfilled, and unthreatened. He is physically, mentally, and emotionally healthy. He has the Power and pride and self-assuredness that comes with knowing and being himself. Habit and convention do not bind him, so he does not experience frustration or stress from want when facing change.

Any addictions or habits the Apprentice has need to be broken. Until then he is not ready to be given full entrustment, because he serves another master. He is not in charge of himself, not free to function as a fully thinking, caring, sensory being if his actions follow uncontrolled dictates. Just as with emotions, habits put him and his People at risk.

The Apprentice journeys beyond his habits through the process of coming to know himself. Childhood patterns, self-concept, and unfulfilled needs play major roles in which habits the Apprentice has, the strength of their control, and whether he even views them as habits. He is blessed with the eye and timely wisdoms of his Guide to carry him through this deeply personal and inevitably painful transition.

When he fully knows himself, he has no more habits. He can then, if he wishes, go back and enjoy for its own sake the object of a former habit. He will experience it differently this time, because something that rules someone cannot be fully fathomed or enjoyed.

Fate and accident have no play in the fortunes of the Guardian. He assumes responsibility for his own life and guides his own destiny. He takes pride in the fact that he is ever alert and in control, ready for any contingency. Having to rely upon his senses, which he has developed to a high state of acuity, he will not consume an intoxicant or other alterative that will compromise his readiness (more in the Alterants chapter of Book II).

He is always conscious of his surroundings, constantly observing. A Civilized Person who speaks with him may think he isn't being attentive to the conversation, because he will not maintain eye contact—he keeps looking around. He is actually very involved in the sharing with his guest, while at the same time he is sensitive on another level to the flow in which he is immersed. His training has taught him to be ever conscious that he is part of something greater than himself, so he is not willing to miss a moment unaware.

Holding awareness through the transitions of the sleeping and awake states seems an impossible task to many, but it is actually quite easy to accomplish when done after the steps through emotions and habits have been taken. The training method is covered in the Sensory Attunement chapter.

A Guardian can be awakened at any time and have immediate composure and a precise sense of place. He will be alert and attuned to his environment, no matter if he was just falling asleep, waking up, or in his deepest sleeptime. He does this by holding on to sleeptime while he is awake, and holding on to awaketime while he is asleep. He is a totally functioning being, having the Powers, Gifts, and awarenesses of both dreamtime and awaketime at his constant disposal.

Brotherhood

A Guardian's service and loyalty to the Greater Good supersedes his commitment to his own People. If ever there is a conflict between the two, he is bound in honor by a powerful pledge to first serve the Greater Good. Even if it appears that he is hurting his People in doing so, he knows that the Greater Good will, in the ultimate, also serve the best interests of his People.

The bond between Guardians is one of undying honor, trust, and service. Guardians of different language and locale regard each other as brothers when they meet, and often they assist each other in their missions. Their bond sneers at the transitory nature of friendships as we know them; it lasts till the life of the flesh walks into the life of that which it next becomes.

Because of the uniqueness of their calling and lifestyle, because of the edge of reality on which they walk, Guardians share a comraderie which draws them together. Hence the formation of Guardian societies. Here the full Power and awareness of the Guardian's Path can be shared with the only others who can feel and breathe it with the same heart.

Contrary to popular Civilized belief, Guardian societies are not secret (nor are those of Healers). In the same way that the mechanics of a healing may be considered miraculous because they cannot be grasped by one who is not initiated into the art, so the way of the Guardian seems mysterious to non-Guardians.

Honor in Conflict

Although a Guardian may be a master of potentially lethal arts, he is seldom a soldier. A soldier serves the self-interest of some individual or group; a Guardian serves the Greater Interest, the Mother-Life, not favoring one life or interest over another. It is only in the Civilized Way that a person is trained primarily to do war.

Battle may or may not play a role in the Guardian's life; if so, it is usually a minor one. Combat training and readiness is part of his Apprenticeship, but not as it exists in the popular stereotype. It has more depth and dimension than just physical combat; he is also trained to do battle against the emotional, psychological, and spiritual threats to his People.

A Guardian treats his adversary with courtesy and respect, no matter how intense the conflict. He does so primarily in honor of the spirit within his adversary, which is also the spirit that dwells within him. He is also aware that having the same Mother, they are brothers.

In fact, he does not have an adversary as we understand the term. His spiritual Path has walked him beyond the dichotomous perspective of this and that, black and white, god and devil. He walks within the realm of Circular Consciousness, where spirit wears no banner and is cloaked in many hues.

He knows that Spirit has many eyes and many hearts in all the forms within which it dwells. And he knows that they all see and feel things in different ways at different times. He knows the seasons of his own eyes and the storms of his own heart and awaits the Balance in their coming and passing before he acts. In the walking of his Journey, he has found that no one person has the clear perception of Spirit, because that which dwells within every person is the *same* Spirit. This is Beauty, and he honors it.

He has found that like begets like, that he will receive as he gives. He will be bathed within the respect he bestows upon his adversary, whether now or at some future time, whether by this adversary or another. As the Circle is ever lapping itself, he may find at their next meeting that he and his adversary are walking together. If that be so, he can hold his head high and greet his brother in pride, knowing that even in conflict he gave his brother nothing but praise and Honor. Besides empowering his character at the time, he is now in turn empowered because his former adversary is free to join him in Honor.

A Guardian is grateful for his adversaries; he does not bemoan or blame them for the difficulties they have brought him. In fact, the more challenging the adversary, the more blessed he feels he is. He has been deemed worthy of such a powerful test and welcomes it. He cries for this Dance that is the reason he walks the Guardian Path. Aware that everything has a purpose, he knows that he will not be given a task beyond his capabilites.

There is no win or lose, as the lessons of the challenge go to both, Honor and pride belong to both. The loser is grateful that he has not been belittled with a weak adversary and is proud that he has been sent one of such Power as a teacher. He will sing in praise of his opponent and gift him for the lesson given. The winner is humbled by being chosen to prevail and takes no advantage beyond that which is his goal and task. Both know that their reason for being is to honor and give service, and both know that they are doing so in winning *and* losing.

In the quiet of the evening, around a Fire,
legends are given life by the voice of a respected Elder.

Children—Our Guardianship

This Journey-step is a beginning for me: With the coming of Zhingakwe's and my son, Wabineshi, I was asked to relearn the old honored ways of Walking in a sacred, balanced manner with children, and to pass this knowledge on to others who are, and will be, blessed with young to Walk beside.

In Family

We are given children to be their caretakers. They are not ours to do with as we choose; they are the sons and daughters of our greater family, of our People, and they are, as we are, children of The Great Mother. Our care of children is on behalf of our People, and as a caring arm of The Mother. When our relations with our children reflect that, we are not alone as parents. The Great Mother's nurturing, the Elder's understandings, and our Culture's traditions are there with us. It is to them that we deliver our children, so it is from them that we gather the heart and hand of their caretakership.

Children are a gift. They are sent to us as teachers; they are the Old Voices coming to us in new face. For those of us who walk in the Civilized Way, they bring back to us the things that were squelched when we left our childhood, such as inquisitiveness, forgiveness, Honor, and wonderment.

Old Way family units are usually larger than their Civilized counterparts. Grandparents and the parents' unwed sisters and brothers are often part of the family. This environment gives children the benefit of adult role models other than their biological parents. They have the opportunity to emulate and be influenced by adults with a variety of interests, perspectives, and character types, which provides for a healthy and growth-stimulating environment.

Grandparents often play a major role in the raising of children, sometimes as primary caretakers. They have the insights and patience that come with years, and they have the time, as they are no longer so involved with material sustenance and service. In some cultures, aunts and uncles who reside outside the family play a significant role also; they may even be known by the children as Mother and Father.

There are no orphans amongst the People. The extended family considers their relatives' children their own and welcome them without qualm or reservation.

Caretaking

We sophomores weren't expected to win our soccer game against the juniors, and we didn't. But it wasn't because we couldn't play better; it's because we played our role. Our starting lineup was comprised of our football and basketball standouts. I was a cross-country runner; I didn't have the rank of those whose sports had cheerleaders and homecoming dances. I started the game on the bench.

By midgame our score showed we had nothing to lose, so a few of us second-stringers were sent in to see some action. After a couple drives, I noticed that we could move the ball effectively up to about mid-field, then we'd lose spirit and just about give it to the juniors. It became obvious to me that there was some kind of unwritten law that we weren't supposed to outperform our upper-classmates—a law I wasn't going to accept.

So on the next three drives I moved the ball upfield to goal position single-handedly, but my team didn't move upfield with the ball to help make the score! I tried a peptalk, telling them that if I could move it upfield alone, think what we could do as a team! They didn't respond, still refusing to cross the invisible mid-field line. The humiliated juniors began "accidentally" kicking and punching me when the refs weren't looking. A play or two later and I was on the bench, sullen and misbelieving. The juniors trounced us, and I'd relearned another lesson in being Civilized.

This experience of mine illustrates one of the major affronts the Civilized Way perpetrates upon its children—peer groups. It commences in earnest at about age six; in short order it squelches the play of imagination, the direction of creative urges, the sound of Voices within, and the sensitivity to external powers and energies. It is the end of their short lives as individuals of Personal Power, and the beginning of their long lives as automatons.

Peer groups encourage children to reinforce in each other the quirks of their age, while at the same time not allowing for the diffusion of its traumas. It magnifies their age-dimensioned view of their reality. Schools are the primary agents in this process. By having children sit, think, walk, and urinate in unison, the schools create citizens suited to the routines of Civilized existence. (Churches, scout and other youth groups, daycare agencies, and other similarly structured organizations also contribute.) The peer pressure this system generates is its own regulating and conforming agent.

Native People encourage their little ones to play with others of varying ages. This gives them the opportunity to emulate older children and to be an inspiration to those younger. They learn responsibility and the skills of caring for and teaching others. Their shared time is a multi-dimensional experience, a microcosm of the life their play is preparing them for.

Native children often are considered shy by an outsider because they do not regularly look others in the eye when speaking to them (reasons given in "A Comparison" section of "The Old Way and Civilization" chapter).

When a Native child enters a room, she usually first travels it with her eyes to acquaint herself with it and its contents. A Civilized child generally goes immediately from place to place to investigate what interests her. This difference comes from the first year of their lives, when Civilized children are allowed to crawl and explore and Native children, in their cradleboards or hammocks, are propped or hung in an advantageous place to observe. This early training in centeredness and observation benefits Native children throughout their lives.

A cradle song from my childhood echoes the days of my ancestral past when our babies knew the cradleboard:

Hush-a-bye, baby, on the tree top,
When the wind blows the cradle will rock;
When the bough bends, the cradle will fall,
Down will come baby, bough, cradle and all.

From the first, the role of the parents is to help their young develop the skills to become independent of them. Parents help best by not doing for their children what they can do themselves, even if it takes them considerably longer and/or they can't do it nearly as well as someone else.

Children of the Old Way are given an environment rich in love and attention. In general, they do not receive physical punishment. With less pressure to conform and more freedom of individual expression than their Civilized counterparts, there is less need for discipline. When it is deemed necessary, it is done within a supportive, caring context. It may take the form of withholding attention or affection, or it may be done by ridicule (see Sensory Attunement chapter).

Children work to create increasing autonomy and space about themselves for two reasons—self-survival and the dispersal of their kind. When children leave the shelter of their parents, they serve these needs best if they've developed the wherewithal to prosper on their own wits within the context of the common good, and to find new places to colonize or introduce the Gifts of their ancestry. In doing so they most effectively strengthen and contribute to their community.

When Civilized People label their youth as rebellious, disobedient, and strong willed, they are using subjective terms that show their cultures' lack of Respect and lack of engendering of the natural, beautiful, and necessary yearnings that aid their youth in becoming fully empowered, independent adults. These terms speak of the judgementalism and repression their children walk with, and of the inadequacy and guilt they feel for their inner yearnings.

Children choose the safest, easiest place to work on developing their autonomy and attempt to do it with adults they trust. Although guiding a child's drive to independence can be challenging, it is a compliment and an Honor to be chosen to do so.

By choosing to be an active participant in their children's searchings, parents and their families are less likely to fall into the role of victim. The trusted parent can draw parameters-boundaries within which their children can choose what, when, and how to stretch their limits, express themselves, and release emotions in ways that are safe for them and not disruptive to those around them.

In balanced relationships with trusted parents (and other adults) of the other sex, children learn how to establish their identities, express themselves, and eventually be mates and/or friends with those of the other sex. Playing this role well allows parents to have good relationships with their grown children and gives the children a great chance for healthy relationships with their mates.

Native children live close to the means of their existence and help to provide it. Knowing the necessity and utility of their contributions, they willingly assist. Once when I saw a young girl being asked to help with something she was unfamiliar with, her father took the time to explain its significance, sacredness, and present necessity. Another time I heard a boy who was helping to gather Firewood being told how it would be used to cook supper and keep them warm for the night. He was shown how to give Thanks for the Wood, and it was explained how it was actually The Sun Father who warmed them through the Wood.

In the quiet of the evening, around a Fire, legends are given life by the voice of a respected Elder. Guised as entertainment, they bring teachings to the children. The fluorescence of Fire's coals and the rising of his flamed plume cast a magic-hypnotic trance. His calming, mesmerizing effect and the focal point he provides give the perfect mood and setting for the draw of the heart and the play of the imagination.

They learn early that the Circle is their protection. They imagine being in the center of a Circle when they feel threatened, and they may walk in a Circle to figure out a problem. It helps them to realize that all things are connected, and that they may well come around on their own answer. (For more on children see Healing chapter of Book III.)

Walking the Hoop

During the first half of the second world of their Hoop of Life, (birth to about age six) Native boys and girls receive similar care and guidance. Girls spend considerable time with their fathers, as do boys with their mothers, which gives the balancing influences of the other sex. After age six, they begin to gravitate toward older members of the same sex and become interested in their activities. Parents help by slowly beginning to disassociate themselves from their children of the other sex.

This deliberate distancing encourages children to seek other adults as role models, which helps to encourage multiple parenting and balance the inevitable influence of their parents' expectations and prejudices. It also lessens the shock of a parent's leaving or absence. (In seafaring cultures, for instance, long absences are common.) In the isolated nuclear families that have become the norm for much of the Civilized Way, a parent's leaving is a traumatic episode in the life of the children (as well as the spouse).

Girls enter the Third World of their Hoop (puberty) with their first Mooncycle. This marks their passage into womanhood—one of the most momentous times of their lives. How they conduct themselves at this time takes on great importance, as it is indicative of who they are becoming as individual women. They are the pride of their families and the admiration of their friends as they are initiated into the Moonlodge. There is usually ceremony to mark the event and perhaps the adoption of the clothing and hairstyle of the women of their People.

Boys' passage into manhood is marked less by their physical maturing and more by their performance as men. As with girls, ceremony and assuming some of the role and accoutrements of adults is a central part of their puberty rite. But the most sacred and significant act is the Dream Quest, which gives form and direction to their adult lives (see Vision chapter in Book II). The final marking of passage from beyond is the receiving of their new names (see Naming chapter in Book II), which will accompany them through adulthood.

Walking Back in Childhood

Childhood is the only time Civilized People are allowed to play—to play out their fantasies, to play at being the people they admire and the things and situations that bring them fulfillment and peace. It's O.K. then to listen to voices and speak to things that other people cannot hear or see. They can do and be what their parents won't allow them to do or be when they "grow up."

A journey back to early childhood puts us more in touch with who we really are than anything else we could consciously do. At that time our essential selves were uncluttered and near the surface. Spirit had life and was a constant companion; our eyes were yet clear enough, our throats were yet open enough that they could give sight and voice to the songs within us. Our Ancestors saw again, touched life again through us. The Life-Energy about us found praise and Honor in the clean depth and intensity of our childish ways.

The great Teachers tell us to be as little children. The Birds and the Wind sing us the same message in the way they live their essential Being. Perhaps peace and happiness come to us when we go back to where we left it.

Elders

Wayne Dennis, *The Hopi Child*

Charles Eastman, *Indian Child Life*

Frederic H. Douglas, *Main Types of Indian Cradles* (Denver Art Museum Leaflet 115, Sept. '52)

Sister Inez Hilger, *Chippewa Child Life and its Cultural Background*

Victor F. Lotrich, *Indian Terms for the Cradle and the Cradleboard* (Colorado Magazine, May '41, Vol. XVIII)

Wilfred Pelletier, *Childhood in an Indian Village*

Taro Yashima, *Crow Boy*

Old Way family units are usually larger than their Civilized counterparts.

*At the appointed time he got into the Canoe and tapped the side
with his Medicine Paddle, and away he went into the night sky.*

Elders–Keepers of the Ancestral Voice

The Grandfather and the Canoe

Years ago, long before the People of the Northern Lakes knew the Longknife traders and missionaries, there lived a revered old man in his village on the Lakeshore. He was a Canoemaker of great skill; people from as far as five sleeps away would come to him when they wanted a very special boat.

One night in a Dream, the Seven Grandfathers came to him. They sat in a Circle around the Firepit of his Wigwam, and he passed his Pipe around to each. They smoked in silence. Then he offered them boiled Venison and dried Blueberries, which they also ate in silence.

After a while, the Grandfathers spoke. They told the old craftsman that soon he would be leaving his People, and that he should begin making a special Canoe to carry him on the last steps of his Journey. This Canoe was to be carved from the Rock of the Granite cliffs along the Lake, and a special paddle was to be hewn from the Ash that grows in the nearby Swamp. They drew symbols on a piece of Birchbark that he was to carve on the paddle handle.

When he awoke he was alone, but his food was gone, and the etched Birchbark lay before him. Without saying a word to anyone, he immediately set to work as he was instructed. The hard Stone quickly wore down his tools and made for slow progress. Still, he toiled unceasingly.

At first the villagers didn't make much of his project; they were accustomed to his working diligently at his craft. But after a while they began to talk amongst themselves, wondering if this man who spent his days pounding Stone was still in possession of his mind. Then they started to ridicule him to his face. After the fourth time his labors were derided, he left the village and put up a small Lodge for himself near where he was building the Canoe.

But the children, his constant companions, kept coming. They were fascinated with this wizened man who told them stories about their parents and grandparents when they were children, and of all manner of things of which they knew little but had great interest. They didn't doubt in the least that this Canoe which he was carving from the Rock would float. And, unlike the older villagers, they didn't question how he was going to get such a heavy craft down to the Water.

The Green Season came and went. Then, on the eve of the Sleeping Moon when the leaves were turning, he told the children that the Canoe was done, and that he was going to launch it that night as soon as it turned black.

After the evening meal, the children went down to bid their beloved storyteller farewell. One by one, the adults came also, but they stayed back in the shadows, so as not to betray their curiosity.

At the appointed time, he got into the Canoe and tapped the side with his Medicine paddle, and away he went into the night Sky. The whole village watched as he went higher and higher, until he was amongst the Star People. And there he can be found to this day, because the Grandfathers rewarded him by making him the constellation known to the People of the Northern Lakes as The Grandfather and the Canoe.

Ever since that day, children and Elders have lived together in mutual regard and sharing. The canoemaker lives on in the night Sky to remind the People that their Elders speak a wisdom that comes from beyond them. With a new respect for the Old Ones, the People from that day forward have listened diligently to their counsel and have given them the place of Honor in their lives.

Legends with the theme of the above are found worldwide. This one I learned from Nokomis (Grandmother) Keewaydinoquay, honored Elder and Healer.

The Beloved Ones

The Creek, a Native People of southeastern North America, refer to their men and women of age and wisdom as the Beloved Ones. No statement applies to Old Way Peoples more universally than that their Elders are held in esteem. They are given the places of Honor at Feasts and ceremonies; they are the first to be seated and the first served. They are the first informed and consulted, and, barring dire circumstances, they are the last to suffer privation. In Councils and Talking Circles (see Book II), they are the first to speak, and it is with their permission that others speak.

It is only practical that Elders be so revered; they are the repositories of knowledge and the springs of wisdom for their People. In their sharing, they ensure survival, and they make life richer and easier. They are the link between the generations, bringing the teachings and memories from the Elders of their youth to the children of their children.

Wisdom is the Elders' greatest Gift. It comes only with time, because it is based on knowledge and experience. The more time, the deeper the wisdom. In the sharing of wisdom, the People trust that their Elders will keep the common good in the forefront, because those younger sometimes lack the wisdom to know the difference. The insights the Old Ones have gained and the traditions they breathe don't allow them to do anything other than selflessly serve their People.

Giving respect to those of age is a great equalizer. It restores humility to those who have seen fewer winters but who have accomplished more; and it gives honor to those who have walked long on their Paths but may not have had achievements so readily apparent as those of others.

The Elder has so long ago left the world of the child that a common language and frame of reference would no longer seem to exist. Actually, the sharing common between children still appears to occur between Elders, but it is swift and unspoken, so it goes largely unnoticed. Bridging this comunication gap would seem to take time and concertedness on the part of the Elder, and patience and attention on the part of the child.

Such is not the case, as the legend that begins this sharing illustrates. Children and Elders have a very special and natural relationship with each other—one that is warm, deep, and spontaneous. It's as though they have an intuitive awareness of their importance to each other as the bridge that gives Power and continuity to the life of their People.

If the Civilized Way would again embrace its Elders, perhaps it could rediscover its primal roots and begin to return to The Mother it so long ago abandoned.

IV

Attunement– Stepping Out of Time

Is a Buffalo still a Buffalo when she is corralled and fed hay . . . ? Without attune-ment, our relationship with The Mother can be nothing more than mechanical . . .

Introduction to Part IV

Several turns of the seasons ago, on a drizzly day late in the Green Corn Moon, three friends and I went to gather Birch and Cedar bark from a section of Forest that a Tornado had damaged. The Trees were dying; we wanted to gather as much bark from them as we could so they could go on sheltering, go on living. We would use the bark to make containers and cover our Lodges.

When we arrived, I left my friends to cut bark while I went on to do some other things. One of them had been gathering there with me a couple days earlier, so I felt confident that he could carry on and instruct the others in the craft.

An hour or so later I returned to three less-than- enthusiastic barkers in rain-soaked clothing with a small pile of shredded bark pieces. Without speaking, I stripped off my clothes, walked into the Woods, and reappeared in fifteen minutes with a solid 3 X 6 foot slab of Birchbark and a longer section of Cedarbark.

"I can't believe you just did that!" was written all over their faces. As I slipped back into my dry clothes, I answered their questions. I mentioned that perhaps flowing with The Mother's mood of the day would have brought them to attunement, thus allowing them to perceive a greater range of approaches and choices. Instead of bearing wet sticky clothing while working, they could have enjoyed the rain, then returned to warm, comfortable clothes when finished. I went on to offer that, had they let their intuitions guide them to a likely Tree, then made an Offering (while explaining why they needed bark and humbly asking the Tree to shed hers for them), they might have been gifted.

Attunement, living in a balanced, interconnected flow with our surroundings, is the underlying theme of these writings. Without attunement, our relationship with The Mother can be nothing more than mechanical, and our sensory, mental, and spiritual awarenesses will remain undeveloped. The attuned individual is totally awake, vibrant, and fully absorbed in the moment's experience. The dancing eye can see more sharply, the perked ear can hear more clearly, the open heart and flowing emotions can embrace more fully. The natural realm begs attunement; without it, that realm would eventually literally reject us—spit us out and send us back to Civilization. We walk our Journeys not so much to find life's meaning as to find its richness and fullness. These are the gifts of attunement.

In the rest of this volume, we dwell on inner attunement—on striking a balance amongst the forces, minds, senses, and graces whose Talking Circle is our Heart-of-Hearts. Book III is strictly our exploration of outer attunement—the respectful way we walk, nourish, and care for ourselves in Balance with the Greater Circle.

The rain had become a light mist by the time my visitors had arrived at the trailhead. They were a family who had come from the city to spend a day with me at my Wigwam camp. Being late afternoon, we decided to head out immediately without waiting for it to dry up. The trail was wet walking, as the Ferns and overhanging branches were heavy with moisture.

As is my custom, I brought up the tail of the troupe. A few paces down the trail, someone glanced back and found me with the bulk of my clothes in my pack. I suggested they all follow suit (or unsuit), but their conventions were strangers to reason. When we reached camp, I redonned my garb and started a Fire to refresh them, as their spirits were nearly as sodden as their clothes.

(The story has a happy ending: This family has begun Walking the wondrous Path toward Balance, and they're a pleasure to be with as we share our growing experiences.)

Sensory Attunement

When I was young, I would closely observe those I admired, to see if I could pick up some clues as to why they were so comfortable in the Woods. They had an easy way with the little irritations that kept me fidgeting. When the Campfire smoke blew my way, I'd end up trying to get out of its reach while nursing burning eyes and throat, while they took it in such stride that I barely noticed their reaction. They seemed to welcome the smudge; they merely squinted and exhaled to keep it from irritating them.

While I wrinkled my brow and swatted at Mosquitos, they were obviously at peace with the buzzing blood siphoners, thankful for their presence and happy to share some space and a few corpuscles with them. As I bemoaned the heat or the cold or the snow, they revelled in the blessings of The Mother's changing tempers. I tolerated the camp food, patiently awaiting my next in-town meal, while they showed respect for the foods' source and preparers and relished its eating. I was ever talking and distracted; they were quiet and attentive to everpresent voices and unfolding lessons.

Not until I was able to spend some periods of time with attuned people did I begin to understand that the mysteries of attunement lie deeper than mere observation could reveal. I learned and grew from those early observations of others, but they were sometimes deceptive. I strove to emulate those who showed such obvious Woods savvy, judging and sometimes deifying them in the process. I focused on the people rather than what was speaking through them. In doing so, I was often captivated by charismatic sorts who gave flashy demonstrations of surface attunement—heady stuff for an impressionable boy.

This was not attunement as I eventually grew to know it. The lessons of attunement were in the smoke and in Mosquito and in Her tempers—not in Peoples' reactions to these things. The Civilized Person *reacts*—looks for and tries different approaches until one works; The Native person *acts*— observes, attunes, and visualizes, then proceeds. It is like the rambunctious explorations of a puppy as compared to the studied, deliberate approach of a Cat.

We learn to act rather than react by becoming fully aware; the method is attunement of all the senses. Doing so is existing beyond our physical bounds, because our senses carry us into the flow in which we are immersed. It is then possible to feel that we are directing ourselves rather than being controlled by our environment.

Occasionally I meet someone who thinks we do not have very sharp senses as compared to many other animals. Of course, there is no comparing our hearing ability with that of Fox, who can detect the unsnapping of my knife sheath at 100 yards. But Deer, who many think to be quite sharp, is actually about average in sight and hearing. After a short time of practice in reawakening our senses, it is not all that hard to get close enough to touch a Deer.

Civilized People have lost the effective use of several of their senses and are no longer aware of the existence of several others. They rely primarily on sight, to a lesser degree on hearing, and very little on smell. Their restricted-environment rational-linear lives are audio-visually based. Still, they could get along better without sight or hearing than they could without touch, balance, and timing—the primary senses.

People of the Old Way lead multi-faceted lives that are rich in adventure and involvement. They rely upon the sophisticated and complex interplay of all their well-attuned senses. Involved in a constant exchange of information, these senses make them marvellously sensitive and efficient sensory beings.

This sensory integration gives Native People a world quite different from the one that is perceived through only two dominant senses by Civilized People. They are senses of observation, which often work separately and disjointedly, whereas the sensory network of Old Way Peoples is one of movement, which causes their senses to be stimulated and function together. Sight and hearing are associated with the conscious, rational mind; the full range of senses integrates the conscious with the subconscious and intuitive.

We can reawaken our own senses, bringing them to a level of attuned sharpness and integration that will give us a new vision of the Circles of our lives. It will bring a sense of wonder and depth to what is now commonplace. Through this chapter winds a path to that reawakening. After an exploration of each of the senses, there will be exercises designed to help renew that sense. Do the exercises as quietly and gracefully as possible. Then as we integrate the lessons of those exercises, our lives' activities will also become quiet and graceful.

The Civilized Person has a tendency to identify her center as being her head; the Old Way Person has two centers—a physical center in his gut, just below the navel, and an overall center in his Heart-of-Hearts. For the following exercises involving movement, let us concentrate on our gut being our center. Being the center of our physical weight, and therefore our balance center, consciously relating to it as such will give our movements more ease and fluidity.

Before beginning a movement exercise, let us rub our hands vigorously together until they're warm and tingly. Then place one palm on the abdomen (just below the navel), and place the other on the small of the back. If we close our eyes for a few minutes and think about the area between our hands as being our center, this awareness will remain with us throughout the exercise.

There is no preparation needed for the non-movement exercises, as they will naturally draw us to our Heart-of-Hearts.

Along with the following exercises, let's remember the complementary role of our Guide. He will have things to offer from his own perspective, especially when we hit impasses.

Intuition

One warm, grey afternoon in the Moon of the Falling Leaves, Talks With Loons and I went to visit a Cherokee family who lived nearby. When we arrived, Running Fox was out in the field target practicing with his bow. In a short while he came in, having just lost his last arrow in the tall, matted Grass. We offered to help him look for it.

Before we got within sight of the target area, Talks With Loons walked off from us at an angle, stopped, and pulled the arrow out from deep under the Grass.

Running Fox still talks about the incident to this day.

Early in my own apprenticeship, when I first saw such beautiful displays of attunement, I rationalized that they were based on acute sensory perception. Eventually, I learned how little I knew. They were not displays; they were actually modus operandi—normal everyday occurrences for those so attuned. And their source was deeper than I perceived it to be. I grew to accept that what Running Fox and I witnessed was no more or less than the Song of a woman whose entire being was sensitized to her Circle, which danced within her even as she danced within it.

Finding that arrow was obviously based (at least in part) on some sort of perceptual sense, but I didn't see any indication of functioning senses in the search. I learned that this phantom sense that guided Talks With Loons was what Civilized People referred to (sometimes derogatorily) as Intuition.

Some people refer to Intuition as the sixth sense, but I consider it to be the first, as it is the most primal of our senses. Animals with none of the evolved sensory organs such as we have still have Intuition. Our other senses grew from Intuition, to further elaborate upon its input. And our other senses short-circuit and feed us disjointed information if they do not remain rooted in Intuition.

Once, to my surprise, Talks With Loons asked me to test her Intuition. I took her to an area unfamiliar to her, blindfolded her, then led her into the brush, spun her around, and asked her to find the nearest nest.

She turned slowly in a Sunwise direction, making a full circle. Then she continued turning, stopping about one third of the way into her second circle. In the direction she was now facing, she took a few steps and pointed to a clump of Grass at her feet. I opened the clump, and there lay an empty Rabbit nest.

This is the one and only time Talks With Loons allowed me to test her. She told me it was not intended to be a test, and it should not be construed as a game, but rather as a glimpse from beyond her into the realm of my own unfolding Personal Power. She went on to explain that if we are exhibitionistic with our Personal Powers, we dishonor spirit and run contrary to the state of attunement that brought them to us, thereby risking losing them.

I faced a burning dawn when I realized that I could not study, could not practice, to do what Talks With Loons did. When it comes, it seeps softly into one's days like silver hairs do on the head of an Elder. Like those hairs, it comes with wisdom and growth, and it comes without awareness or celebration to mark its appearance.

Today, when I see younger Seekers frustrated and impatient with their progress, as I was, my memory draws deep to those early days and I feel again what they feel. Even more than in my day, they are stepping out of a world of canned and immediate me-gratification. A display of Intuition fireworks would encourage and titillate them, but a Guide dare not do that. It would bring them to the edge of their seats waiting for the next display rather than settling back to explore the less dazzling, but more profound, depths of the night sky.

On the average, we need a full turn of the seasons to begin grasping an awareness of the dimension behind the fireworks of Intuition. Then, when we are able to walk into the depths of that dimension and look back, the fireworks will be as one of many, many stars instead of spanning the entire sweep of our vista. Until that time, our dedication and patience with these exercises will help carry us. Then we also can begin to hear the voice of a lost arrow and the voice of a Rabbit nest. During the time until this Moon comes around again, know that Squirrels and Wind and Stars all await our stepping into the Dance where we all turn together.

Intuition Exercises

As I've already mentioned, there are no exercises we can practice to empower our Intuitive Sense, but we can practice at opening the channels so that we can consciously hear its voice.

The voice of Intuition is known variously as superconsciousness, guardian angel/spirits/animals, the Holy Spirit. I prefer to call it the second awareness. The first awareness we have already explored—being fully present and intimately attuned to the flow within the current instant. The second awareness is being aware of ourselves being aware; it is being our own observer, our own second perspective.

It's actually fairly easy, as most of us do it already from time to time. After you've made a mistake, have you ever said, "I knew I was doing it wrong while I was doing it, but I went ahead and did it anyway." That "knew" was your second awareness.

The second awareness gives us the greater picture, the overview. It is not bound by the pattern of our habits or the conventions of our existence. In a conscious effort to get things done, or to keep doing things the way we're used to doing them, Civilized People usually discount that second, little, nagging voice. After a while, they can hardly hear it. I call this block between the first and second awareness the *Veil*.

Lifting the Veil just takes practice; there is no special skill involved. When you hear the voice, stop everything and give it conscious recognition to empower it. Then follow the voice. Every time you give it conscious power, you make it easier to lift the Veil the next time, as you are strengthening the channel between intuition and consciousness. (If the Veil is heavy and you are not hearing the voice, the Veil will lighten by practicing the form of meditation given in the Circle Attunement chapter.)

There are two pitfalls to watch out for in beginning to function from the second awareness: One is the habit of listening to it in retrospect rather than in the moment, which keeps us going back, trying to re-do the past by correcting our errors. The other is not maintaining a balance between the two awarenesses by allowing the second awareness to dominate. We are intuitive beings, but we are also rational beings, and it takes practice to bring the two voices in balance to our Heart-of-Hearts.

The seeming conflict arises when the cultivated skills or modes of functioning of the first awareness are immediately appropriate, but the second awareness suggests a different action based upon its grander perspective. For example, imagine that I am sliding through a Boulder-strewn rapids in my canoe and I need to make a quick move to avoid kissing a Rock. My second-awareness impression would likely be to challenge my reflexes and test the limits of my skill by getting as close as possible to that Rock. On the other hand, my first awareness suggestion would be to exercise caution, to use the tried-and-true techniques that have gotten me around many Rocks before.

More often than not I would operate from my second awareness in a situation like this, because it would be for the Greater Good—it would keep me growing and adaptable. But this time it would be a mistake, because I'm returning to camp with several baskets full of Medicinals that I just gathered and wish to keep dry.

Choices such as the one in the above example do not occur after one has permanently lifted the Veil. Rather, the Heart-of-Hearts considers information such as the above, and more, and directs the appropriate action.

It is imperative that we have a well-attuned first awareness before we seriously begin lifting the Veil to Intuition. Attempting to juggle two dysfunctional awarenesses is courting disaster; we could be placing ourselves and others in jeopardy. Imagine the above canoeing scenario with the added variable of the voice of both awarenesses being unreliable.

Expect errors in judgement as you progress. In fact, welcome them and give thanks for their occurrence, because they are powerful personal teachers.

The Primary Senses

There are three senses that spring directly from Intuition—Touch, Shadowing, and Balance. They are primary because they were the first to evolve and specialize from intuition, they are the first to function in a baby, and they are the senses a person can do least without. Like intuition, we have no conscious, intellectual involvement with them. Our spontaneous actions result from them, and they are the basis of all motion and sensuality.

In the natural realm, the primary senses are indispensable; they're extraneous to the time-and-structure oriented aspects of Civilization. Only a few percent of its Peoples' sensory input comes from these senses, as they are largely nonfunctional. They have atrophied from disuse at an early age.

The same is true of our domestic animal kin, as they have been bred to function within the same structured and regimented form of existence as Civilized People. However, the primary senses of animals are less repressed than in People, because animals' rational-linear thought processes play a lesser role in their mental functioning. Domesticated wild animals are also affected, but because they have not been genetically manipulated, they retain more of their primary sense function.

Exercising the primary senses can resuscitate them, the process actually causing the brain to change and become more sensually responsive. When exercising, it is important to remember that our emotional state affects the primary senses, so in turn affects the brain's regenerative changes. (This is because both emotions and primary senses are so closely related to intuition that they affect each other.)So if necessary, take time to enter a balanced emotional state before commencing the following exercises.

Touch

As Talks With Loons and I reached the edge of the Prairie opening, Father Sun's intense, hazy presence was just about to slip behind the treetops. Talks With Loons suggested that we come to this spot to perform a special meditation to The Sun Father at this time of the Blueberry Moon, when He is at His most powerful. She said this meditation would become a Song of Oneness if done along with the day becoming night.

Without speaking, she took off her shirt. I equated this with a sure case of anemia at best, and a suicide request at worst, because Mosquitos were already beginning to swarm around us in the lengthening tree shadows.

But I had long before learned that with Talks With Loons, things are often enough not what they seem. So I removed my shirt and relaxed into whatever was to follow.

As we faced The Father to let Him burn into our eyes to become our light, the massing horde commenced to cover my skin (and, I assumed, hers). But I dared not show my discomfort by breaking my posture. Even if it wasn't a ceremony, my pride still wouldn't allow me to show my limitations in front of her, because she had already shown me how to live in Balance with Mosquitos.

I sensed that she knew this and was using it as a tool to bring me to a threshold. I knew and trusted her intuitive sense about such things, as many times before she had seen the direction of my Path when I could not and guided me appropriately.

All my energy was directed at getting from one second to the next. My skin burned and itched like it never had before; my reflexes tore against my determination to be silent and accepting. I felt a lifetime of agony and spent a lifetime of self-control in those few minutes.

Then the Veil was lifted: The last rays of Sun glowed golden-warm inside my eyelids and spread to my toes and fingertips. I became my pain, embraced it, and soared through it. I thanked my teachers and asked more of them to land upon me. My smile must have swallowed my face as I flowed into Sun's forever glow and painted the Clouds and Treetops.

Like the other primary senses, Touch is complex and deep-rooted. It gives us the feeling not only for temperature and pressure changes, but also for movement. The skin would seem to be our obvious touch organ: however, the responses of muscles, bones, joints, and other organs work in unison with skin to give us the sense of Touch.

When we move, our sense of Touch helps us to automatically adapt to the ever-changing situation. For example, when the wind pushes us, we lean into it, or when we trip, we extend our arms to catch ourselves.

Deep in the night Woods, a group of Seekers were sitting in a semi-circle around their Elder, who was talking about things unseen, voices our ears could not follow. As the night progressed, it grew cool, dropping to around 50°. My comrades were wearing jackets and sweaters; I was bareback.

When we broke the Circle to turn in, a woman asked me, "Aren't you cold?" "Yes." "Doesn't it bother you?" "No." I was cold, and I was comfortable with it, because I accepted it. In fact, it added to the dimension of that evening, sharpening my presence and awareness. I felt that my acceptance of the cold helped to provide a connection between the reality that touched me and the more ethereal reality of which my Elder spoke. Insulating myself from that Touch may have isolated me from the connectedness I experienced.

To fear cold is to fight cold and, ultimately, be defeated by it. When we resist cold, we create a situation of imbalance, forcing ourselves to try to maintain a comfort level not attuned to our surroundings. We shiver, and our perceptual awareness dulls as we became absorbed in our plight.

Acceptance of the cold allows our bodies to attune themselves and adjust to it. By allowing the cold to embrace us, and in turn embracing the cold, we become friends with the cold, we become the cold.

Touch Exercises

Toddlers and babies are great Teachers of Touch. Observing them shows us what we could be, as their primary senses are fully functioning. This is true of Civilized babies as well; their primary senses are not suppressed until they reach 4 to 6 years of age.

Babies have retaught me the importance of the mouth and nose as Touch organs. After exploring an object with their finger, it will often go into the sensitive mouth to gain further information about it. They use their nose to detect heat and cold, as it is more sensitive than fingertips.

Our very young have more beautiful things to share with us besides how to Touch again; spending relevant time with them as we walk our Journeys will bring us many wisdoms.

Trying to detect our individual pulse rates in as many ways and places as possible is a challenging exercise that can involve sight and hearing as well as Touch. Find a quiet place, strip your clothing, and have a notebook handy to record the spots where you've found your pulse. Have a separate column for each sense you use. You'll undoubtedly be quite surprised (and impressed) with the length of your list, and where you can find your pulse. And you'll have a lot of fun comparing lists with others!

Come back to this exercise from time to time as your sensual acuity sharpens, and you'll be able to further add to your list. (Hint: changing position changes perspective, as also does time of day, weather, emotional state, and energy level.)

Cold is intimidating to many people—so much so that some of us miss the gifts of the turning seasons by trying to avoid it. This is unfortunate, because cold is quite easy to adapt to—much easier than heat.

Some of this adaptation is attitudinal, as already discussed, but most of it is physiological. Our bodies will naturally acclimatize as cold weather approaches. However, the largely indoor lives that most of us lead don't provide us with enough exposure to cooler temperatures to trigger this process. We must touch the cold in order to become it.

In so doing, I've found a way to estimate the temperature. If, when breathing in through my nose, the moisture inside it lightly freezes, the temperature is 5° F. The faster and harder the moisture freezes, the lower the temperature. Experiment to see if this works for you and discover what temperature corresponds to the rate and degree of freezing you experience. A consistent rate of inhalation is important for an accurate basis of comparison.

My favorite cold-caressing exercise is what I call *sleeping cold*. It involves nothing more than sleeping with one blanket less than normal. For instance, if I usually use three blankets, I will now use two, or if I usually use one blanket, I will now sleep with just a sheet. Sleeping cold gradually raises the metabolic rate, which generates more heat, and it constricts the surface capillaries, thereby cutting down blood flow and resultant heat loss.

We need to sleep cold for about three weeks in order to effect these changes; continuing to sleep cold will assure that they are maintained for the season. I sleep cold year round to decrease my risk of hypothermia due to exposure, and to be in condition for summer swimming in cold water. I also sleep better when I'm cool; my bedroom window is open year round.

The beauties of this exercise are that it can be done by anyone, any-where, it requires no effort, and there are healthy fringe benefits, such as a more efficient metabolism and the burning of fat.

Here are a few additional hints for keeping warm:

— Wear layered clothing, which allows easy adjustment to avoid overheating and chills. Sweating is dangerous, as sweat-soaked clothing can lead to severe chilling. So avoid absorbent fabrics like cotton and use wool, which resists saturation and retains warmth even when wet.

— Don't repress shivers, as they generate body heat. When not moving, Cat-stretching (see Book III) can be used to keep warm.

— Oily skin retains heat better than dry skin. Applying oil or fat to exposed skin makes a noticeable difference in cutting heat loss.

— A small portion of the body exposed will wick heat from the entire body. Wearing vests and going without head covering are not recommended.

Chapped lips are a common cold-weather problem. Saliva is the best lip balm; get in the habit of periodically licking your lips and they won't chap. Or, if they are already chapped, they will heal quickly. A thin coating of oil or fat will help to keep lips from drying but should not be used on already-dry lips until they are rehydrated. (Zhingakwe has a handy lip balm—she rubs her lips across my forehead to coat them in natural skin oil—the best thing for them.)

In below-freezing weather I often run barefoot, in just a pair of shorts, and I sometimes work and ski bareback. I'd be uncomfortably warm if I tried to wear more. What is considered cold is relative; friends from the South think my environment is cold, while I take our White Season to be mild and short in comparison with that of those who dwell further north.

Even more so than cold, heat is a powerful and unrelenting adversary if not welcomed and embraced. Its extremes are more challenging to find Balance with than those of cold.

As with cold, we can attune ourselves to heat with exposure. Our skin capillaries enlarge and our blood circulation increases bringing body heat to the surface where it radiates away. Eating seasonal indigenous foods aids in this process, as their mineral salt ratios encourage capillary dilation. (In contrast, indigenous northern foods help restrict capillaries.)

Sweating, which cools us by evaporation, is our most obvious adaptation to heat. High humidity slows evaporation, which causes us to feel hotter, and extreme sweating can lead to dehydration.

Dark people have an advantage in hot climates; their skin pigment and hair intercepts Sun's rays before they can penetrate and radiates the heat back to the environment.

As can be seen, our adaptations to touching heat are incomplete. If we are light skinned, eating alien foods, spending most of our time in controlled environments and/or living in humid areas, we could have trouble befriending Sun's gift when we spend time outdoors. Following are some suggestions to help kindle a more compatible relationship, which were given to me mostly by Native animals who walk in Balance with The Sun Father.

— Lay low. Hug the shade in midday, saving activity for the coolness of morning and evening. Along with ducking the hottest part of the day, inactivity saves us the additional heat generated by movement. Also, midday is the time of maximum sunburn risk, and skin so damaged does not sweat well. Take particular note concerning children, because they sweat less than adults, so already have a harder time reducing body heat.

— Eat lightly. Food is fuel; when it burns, it creates heat. Eat less, and avoid rich and heavy foods.

— Drink heavily. Waiting till you're thirsty means your body fluids are running up a deficit, so drink regularly. Avoid salt and sugary drinks; water and local juices are best.

Shadowing

I watched a vixen Fox move her cubs from a den in a low bank beside a marshy Stream to a higher one atop a glacial ridge. That evening a Thunderstorm came close to flooding the lower den.

Curious as to whether or not her den switching was coincidental to the Storm, I watched her again when the next heavy Rain was forecast. She did the same thing, moving the cubs back to her preferred lower den after the Water subsided. Both times she acted hours before any sign of weather change that I could detect.

I witnessed this inspiring display of the Shadowing sense when I was ten years old. At the time, I had but the faintest glimmerings of the powers of Intuition; the she-Fox was the first to present herself and offer to Guide me into the realms of sensory attunement.

Shadowing is the sense that regulates our functioning within time. A healthy Shadowing sense keeps us so close to the present that we are its shadow, hugging it precisely, moving synchronously with it, never leaving it. Our various rhythms, such as mood and awake/sleeptime, are regulated by shadowing. Perhaps more than any other, the functioning of this sense distinguishes Civilized from Old Way People.

The Shadowing sense determines whether time goes fast or slow, whether we are happy or depressed. If time drags and living isn't much fun, our Shadowing sense is dysfunctional; if we experience recurring depression, our Shadowing sense is virtually non-functional. It is functional and healthy if time flies and life is light and enjoyable.

Time and pleasure are so closely related that we do not subconsciously distinguish them. So if we live in the moment, we are happy; if we do not live in the moment, we are not. It's really as simple as that. Adjusting our internal clock so that the only time it shows is now is the key to bliss.

I've asked numbers of Civilized People of various creeds, professions, and economic levels if they were truly happy, and only a few could sincerely say they were. What a tragedy to walk this life without happiness! Following are exercises with power to nurture the Shadowing sense in all of us who live the Civilized Way and Walk this Journey together. My fervent Song of desire is that through the gifting of these exercises, we will return to joy.

Shadowing Exercises

Simbut Meaxtkao (Mohican for Silver Wolf) began to teach me shadowing exercises while she was still a suckling pup. Unlike my Husky pups, who would get totally lost in playing with me, she maintained a sense of autonomy and perspective that clearly spoke of something she knew about play that I didn't. At first I thought she was aloof with me because she was a Wolf, and I was Civilized. That didn't turn out to be the case; I watched her with her siblings and they acted with each other in the same manner that she acted with me.

The Wolf pups studied each other intently, their games of chase and tag getting more complex the better they learned to "shadow" each other. Soon they were anticipating each others' moves. They were getting so good at catching each other that it looked like there was soon not going to be much sport to the game anymore.

Then their Shadowing took on another level of complexity—the chased began skipping their next planned move to throw the chaser off kilter, and the chasers, anticipating the next move of their quarry, halted their pursuit and cut over to meet their quarry where that move took them. They were Prophet-Shadowing— predicting the event to follow the event currently being shadowed.

Simbut was so much more clever than me, in short order, she had me flawlessly Prophet-Shadowed. When I no longer felt her at my heels, I knew she was going to be waiting for me right where my supposedly deceptive dodgings were bringing me. I felt like a Mouse being played with by a Cat. If she had the desire to play organized sports, she'd quickly dominate.

Reflex—responding to an event *after* its occurrance, lies on the other side of Shadowing from Prophet-Shadowing and could be viewed as its opposite. For the Civilized, including non-Humans, reflex is usually all that remains of the Shadowing sense. Reflex is Shadowing's crudest expression; no matter how sharpened our reflex, it is still a *re*action to the moment rather than synchronous movement within the moment. So reflex cannot bring timelessness, i.e. bliss.

As my tutelage under my Wolf kin continued, I came to realize that conscious rational processes were too slow to be the basis of their Shadowing. I reasoned that strategies and movements of such foresight and synchronicity would be seated in a lower brain—one that has the wisdoms of Shadowing intrinsic to its makeup and is common to all beings who Shadow.

That primal brain, in combination with sharply attuned senses and primed physiques, gave the mystical air to the Wolves' movements. Their rational brains were only a crossroads—a synthesizing point—for that which came from deeper within, and without, them.

I never did get as good as the Wolves, but I did eventually become a challenge for them. I did so by first joining them in the Earth-consciousness state (see Spiritual Attunement chapter) then letting myself get wild 'n crazy with them, not worrying about how silly I looked or how well I was doing.

It was infectious—the more I allowed myself oneness with them, the more I heard what they heard. Our play became as though it were happening in slow motion; I had plenty of time to anticipate their next moves. In as smoothly as we moved within each others' movements, our play felt (and appeared) as though it were choreographed. In fact, I then knew it no longer as play, but as the lifedance of the Hunt, the eye of the Guardian.

The Wise Ones tell us that in order to know something, we must become it. For instance, in order to know Deer, we must become a Deer. We of the Civilized Way cannot become, because of primal brain functions that went dormant when we abandoned the Old Way. The following three exercises reawaken, nourish, and attune those functions. (They are stressed in the first levels of Guardian training.)

These exercises, though necessarily reactive to begin with, will, with repetition and committed involvement, bring us to the sharp and instantaneous point of nowness. There we can move unfettered by the dimension

of time. In fact, the rewards of these exercises are so great that, as entice-
ment for practicing them, I'll share some of what will come to us.

— Shadow-walking will give our movement the acuteness to become Cat-
like stalkers and trackers, and to automatically adjust to changes in the
environment about us.

— Shadowtalking will give us the ears to hear the words of People (Humans and otherwise) and the Elements, at the same instant they are
uttered, and eventually, to hear those words *before* they are uttered
(Prophet-Shadowtalking). Or even if they are not uttered. It will also
bring us super-learning skills; we'll learn new languages quickly and
sing along right away to new songs.

— Shadowmiming will bring us quick physical rapport with others. It will
help us to express our body language and sensitize ourselves to that of
others. And it will bring us superior performance in such interactive
activities as dance, contact sports, and martial arts.

Some folks (usually in the Fourth World of their Hoop of Life) feel
awkward with these exercises, particularly Shadowtalking. They feel that
it is a breach of privacy, a threat to their autonomy. I felt the same at that
age, but it really didn't matter; those who gave me these exercises were
practicing on me whether I consented or not. In fact, I wasn't aware that
they were doing anything. When I was let in on the secret, I was the loser
for my stubborn refusal to participate. They read me at will, and I stayed
righteously ignorant (and unattuned). I didn't grasp what "becoming a
Deer" meant.

Shadow-walking

Our shadows know us perfectly, mirroring our every move, every nu-
ance and peculiarity. No matter how fast or slow we move, or how hard
we try to outsmart them, they unfailingly occupy the precise space beside
us. Our goal in this exercise is to become as attuned to something's movements as is its shadow.

As with all three of these exercises, we begin by Coming to Oneness.
In extending our consciousness to the circle in which we flow, we free
ourselves to move within its rhythm rather than being bound and limited
by our own.

Then find a group of tall plants or a small Tree swaying in the Wind,
and stand so that your shadows mingle. Become a sister Tree, rooting
yourself, stiffening your lower trunk and leaving your upper trunk more
flexible to sway with its branches. Raise your arms so that their shadows
become as the branches' shadows.

Attune yourself to the cues that foretell when and how the Tree will sway—the sight and sound of distant tree tops catching the Wind, the light gust that laps your Tree just before the main gust. Watch the nearby ground cover and dress sparsely so that you can feel the countercurrents that affect the lower branches differently than the upper.

Now, dance with the Winds. Gauge your increasing attunement by how synchronously your tree-shadow is moving with the Tree's shadow. Pay particular attention to the nuances of movement, such as a branch in countersway to the trunk, or leaves rustling in one part of the Tree but not another.

When you become as graceful and responsive as Tree, do the exercise blindfolded, with an observer gauging you. (Blindfolding is necessary because we subconsciously still rely on the potential of our eyes to help us if we merely close them.)

Anything that moves can be Shadow-walked; be inventive. You can now begin practicing the most difficult exercise—Shadow-walking your own kind. You'll need a cooperative but unaware partner, as you'll be slipping in unannounced behind her and shadowing her every move and gesture.

Shadow her closer and closer as you improve, striving to become her second skin. Intersperse your Shadowing attempts with observation, noting the peculiarities of her stride and posture changes that foretell shifts in direction and speed.

The goal is to slip in and out of your partner's shadow without detection, and to be as tight and accurate a shadow as possible. When you're becoming proficient at that, add a level of complexity by asking your partner to do abrupt and unexpected moves.

Versatility and adaptability are gained by partnering with different people, and depth of awareness comes with switching roles and being shadowed.

Practice regularly until you have confidence and ability to undetectedly Shadow strangers at your whim. At this point, a Veil will lift; you'll be able to begin envisioning not only the maker of a track, but also the maker's weight, height, sex, health, emotional disposition, and intellectual preoccupation. And you'll be able to envision the track someone will make by observing them. You're now ready to begin your training as a tracker/stalker (see Book III).

Shadowtalking

As the above brought physical attunement with others, this exercise brings intellectual attunement.

Our echo is our voice's shadow. But it is like a reflex in that it is not a direct and instantaneous mirroring. Our goal in Shadowtalking is to be another person's echo, to bring it back to him across the lapse of time so that his echo is as his voice.

Begin by simply mimicking other people as they talk (*consenting* people, as some find it extremely irritating). You'll make rapid progress at closing the time-gap between your voice and his, then you'll plateau out and not be able to get any closer. This is because you are reacting, using your secondary senses and rational facilities, which necessitates some time for input synthesis and response. (This reactive process will be sidestepped in the next level of this exercise; the purpose for initially using it was to give us an easy, already familiar way to be accustomed to mimicking.)

Only by stepping inside the person we are Shadowtalking can we have the premonition as to what he is about to say, and at what pace, volume, and inflection he is going to say it. Because of this, Shadowtalking will be the most challenging sensory attunement exercise for most of us. It will likely take many turns of the seasons of diligent practice and observation before we can Shadowtalk on the level of an Old Way person.

Besides the fact that we must retrain our minds to function from primary rather than secondary senses, Shadowtalking takes time because the knowing of others comes with the wisdom of age. But that is not to say that we cannot make encouraging and ongoing progress from the beginning. There are some fairly easily readable cues that foretell the voice to follow:

Before someone speaks, his eyes become directed, his head raises and posture straightens, a breath is taken, lips purse and take form. Body language begins to talk before a word is uttered. Whether he is responding to a question, expressing a need, or reacting to his environment, he gives indications as to what he will say. His eyes blink faster if the feeling he is about to express is negative, slower if positive. His practical vocabulary in everyday usage is a small fraction of his functional vocabulary, which, in short order, gives bounds to his possible word choices. He is a creature of habit, repeating the same words, phrases, thought sequences, and reactive patterns, even though the subject matter may change.

Begin by paying strict attention to, and noting, these cues. Soon you'll be subconsciously picking them up, spending less and less time on them to attune yourself.

Anything that makes a periodic sound can be Shadowtalked. For example, I've practiced on Dogs and ticking clocks. My favorite is the sound that comes from a distant source that can be seen before heard, such as a steamwhistle's escaping steam. The important point is to practice on a variety of things, thus expanding and deepening your skill.

Perhaps the most potent gift of Shadowtalking is that only truth is heard, no matter what is spoken. Once we can truly walk within another's footsteps and speak with his breath, we know his words, and their substance, whether or not they are uttered.

Native People (Human or otherwise) are natural Shadowtalkers; not speaking from heart with them is wasted energy, and shallow. The Civilized sometimes deride Natives as being childlike and trusting, not knowing its ultimate virtue or that that is all they can be.

Shadowmiming

This exercise attunes us emotionally to others.

A mirror is the epitome of Shadowmimers, meticulously duplicating the unfolding of a smile, the birth of a tear. Having no feeling of its own, and being precisely attuned to that which is before it, the mirror, to an observer, could just as well be the source as the Shadower:

We, having depths of feeling and tradition to step beside in order to Shadowmime, don't have it as easy as a mirror. Nor do we have it as easy as an actor, the best of whom are mimes, but not Shadowers. However, as giving is receiving, there are rewards in the striving that are unavailable to the mirror or the actor.

This will be the easiest of the three Shadowing exercises for most, as Coming to Oneness is the only requirement to leaving our conscious identities behind and Shadowing another's. As we grow in depth in Coming to Oneness, we grow as Shadowmimes.

Partner with someone who is expressive and uninhibited. Enter into Oneness, then sit on the floor across from your partner, facing him. Drink in his eyes, the furrows on his brow, the way he breathes, and let them become yours. Feel his agitation with a nearby noise, the sudden mood change that repaints his face.

In time, he will begin to dwell in you. When he sighs, you will feel his sigh within you; when he moves, you will feel compelled to move with him. Perhaps one day a tear will leave your eye just as it leaves his. This will be a sign that you have become a Shadowmime of the caliber of a mirror, as another's personal sadness is most difficult to Shadow.

Fear of losing one's self in another is the biggest impediment to Shadowmiming. Trust in partner not to manipulate or exploit by his presence within you is one way to surmount the fear. Trust in Bimadissiwin— the Lifeforce—is another way, it allows you your partner's gift of self without suspicion of his motive or fear of being consumed by his Power.

Practicing each of the three Shadowing exercises concurrently aids progress in all of them, as each nourishes a root of the same tree.

Balance

I watched Deer's spirit leave her as she lay in the light of the car whose speed and direction she misjudged. Reverently taking her gift of flesh and sinew, I hoisted her form to an Oak under the bright Moonlight. In the process of undoing what she had brought together, I sliced my thumb and viewed my own sinew as I opened the gash to bleed and stitch it.

Another time, as I was swinging by my hands through the treetops, the flash of death-awareness riveted me as I crashed through branches on my way to landing on my back on a Rock. Amazed that I was still conscious, much less in little pain, I walked silently home in adrenal-powered wonder as to how I differed from my tree dwelling Ape kin.

Accidents? It may appear at times that our lives are a sequence of fortune, folly, and encounter that occurs as it does by happenstance—by us being either in the right or wrong place at the right or wrong time. But can something in which we are directly and consciously involved be correctly termed an accident? And what about those events that come to us at the times they are needed?

We can view accidents from two levels—physical and flow. The above examples, involving (seemingly) unexpected harm, are physical accidents; those (seemingly) random occurrences in our lives that often end up having significance or purpose are accidents of flow.

Did I slice my thumb or fall accidentally, or did I lose some aspect of Balance and, because of that, tumble or slice myself? Was the she-Deer's death an accident, or was it for my hunger and to return her yet-unborn mutant Fawn to the Deer-Spirit?

If we were each to step back into Circle consciousness, we would doubtless find that our "accidents" were each the result of some lack of Balance in our lives. In the same light, those "accidental" occurrences would be found fitting into a cognizant pattern.

In the Old Way, there are no such things as accidents; there are only physical or flow imbalances. This perspective differs with that of much of the Civilized Way. It allows Native People deliberate involvement in the cause and effect of their lives, and in the lives of others. It also gives recognition to the Rhythm of The All-About, which brings particular happenings to their lives at specific times. Simply put, instead of the Civilized mystery and frustration over accidents is the Old Way awareness of Personal Power and overall purpose.

A Teacher in my youth kept admonishing me to "Walk in Balance", but he never showed me how. He just continued to give my "accidents" back to me in a way that forced me to seek their underlying cause. As the awareness of Balance grew within me, I felt overwhelmed, as when first experiencing a strong, pervasive emotion. I still describe the feeling of being in Balance as akin to a deep awareness of an emotion being experienced.

Notice that I have yet to define Balance. Again, Balance resembles an emotion in that it cannot be adequately put to words, and it cannot be fully understood by someone who has not felt its presence. At best, I can suggest that we have become aware of our sense of Balance when acceptance and a feeling of personal involvement are natural reactions to pain or unplanned occurrences.

There are physical and spiritual aspects of Balance. The physical aspect works in close interaction with our senses of sight, Touch, smell, and hearing; the spiritual aspect, in conjunction with our Shadowing sense, directs our way with time and bliss. A dysfunctional physical aspect causes the illusion of physical accidents; a dysfunctional spiritual aspect brings about the illusion of accidents of flow.

Balance Exercises

There is nothing we can do, *per se,* to regenerate the spiritual aspect of Balance, other than walking our Journey by the Old Way principles contained in this book. However, concerning physical Balance, there is a set of exercises I use to attune myself to better literally *Walk* in Balance.

These exercises address the simplest and most accessible aspect of the Balance sense; in doing so, they enliven the entire sense and open the channels for its full expression.

Prepare yourself for these, our first movement exercises, by reading the Physical Attunement Exercises chapter in Book III. If you can easily keep your balance while standing on one foot with your eyes shut, both on an incline and on the level, you may not need the first exercise.

One-Foot Balance

Just lift one foot, and you're doing it. It's best not to think about it, but to let your Balance sense handle it, because in a natural situation your mind will need to be doing other things and so should not also be burdened with the work of the primary senses.

You'll find that the higher you raise your leg, the more it affects your balance. To vary your center of balance, stretch your leg out in front of you, behind you, beside you. Switch legs. When you find yourself improving, switch your weight to the ball of your foot, your heel, the inner and outer sides of your foot.

Then try uneven surfaces, varying slopes, stream currents, and wind. Vary your approach angles so that your reawakening sense of Balance learns to adapt to changing conditions. For example, when practicing in Wind, choose a place where it is gusty rather than steady, and rotate so that you are being hit on various sides.

Tucking your raised foot behind your opposite knee adds a level of difficulty, because your raised leg is no longer free to help balance. It also adds a psychological level of difficulty, because your free foot is not as readily available to catch your fall.

One of the beauties of this exercise is that it can be done while waiting in line, while doing dishes—anywhere and anytime you are standing. I've been doing it regularly in public for years, and only a couple of people have noticed that I was doing anything out of the ordinary.

A practice field can be made by firmly embedding six-inch diameter log sections within varying stepping distances of each other, so that they are sticking up at various heights of from 3 inches to a foot. While balancing on one log, practice leaning down to pick something up at various distances from you. Practice jumping from log to log, forward, backward, and to the side.

(*Warning*: The log practice field is a sure shin-nicker and ankle-twister for the substantially overweight or those not already adept at one-foot balance. Though barefoot is best, begin by wearing high shoes that give ankle protection *if in doubt of your ability*.)

Walking Balance

When I was a boy, I regularly walked the railroad tracks, as they were the easiest trail to the Woods and swimming. I walked miles on the rails, eventually learning to jump from rail to rail and maintain my balance. After that, crossing a stream over a spanning log was like walking a sidewalk.

You can do the same exercise in your yard by securely staking a two-inch thick plank (narrow side up) or small diameter log so it will not roll. When you're able to stop on command, turn around, walk backwards, and vary your speed, set up two more planks adjacent to yours, one parallel and one perpendicular. Start by staking both planks quite close to your original, and practice switching from plank to plank from a resting position and while moving. Increase the distance between planks as your sense of Balance strengthens.

Blindfold Balance

When you become adept at the above exercises, do them blindfolded. It will add another level of refinement to your blossoming Balance sense. And there are times when you can't count on your eyes, such as in the dark, or when walking in murky Water or through brush. But why a blindfold rather than just closing your eyes? Because even if you don't open your eyes, you're aware that you can at any time. So you don't give full power to your Balance sense. The blindfold eliminates the rational adjunct (eye-forebrain) from the primal translation of inner Balance to outer Balance.

As you will notice, doing the exercises blindfolded is stressful and draining. Until Balance's physical aspect is reattuned, it demands a tremendous amount of inner energy. So it is best to practice blindfolded for only short period at a time. (I'd suggest a 15 minute maximum.)

The Test

Even though you're doing well with the exercises, your newly attuned sense of Balance may let you down when it comes to walking a hogback or crossing a Beaver muckflat on felled Trees. The backyard plank is easy to take to when the only risk is landing on soft turf all of a few inches below! When the risk becomes a dunking in a Stream touched by the Freezing Over Moon, a new variable is added—fear.

It acts as a rational inhibitor to the independent functioning of Balance. When fear takes over, we mistrust our senses and interject mental commands to try to gain rational control. The mind is slow and calculating; it doesn't hold a candle to our senses' speed, precision, and innate grasp of a situation. So we fail. (Fear, how to read it and use it to advantage, is covered in the Seeking Wisdom chapter of this text and in the Healing chapter of Book III.)

To test your Balance sense as related to fear, inject some risk. Set up your plank or log at some elevation above water, or a mudhole, wear good clothes, and see how you do.

A person who walks in the natural way is more comfortable with these exercises and learns quicker. If you're having some trouble, or aren't satisfied with your rate of progress, work on your Deerstepping (in the Earth chapter of Book III) and your physical Balance will improve right along with your walking.

The Secondary Senses

Smell, hearing, and sight require our conscious, rational involvement in their functioning. We could live without one or more of them. They do not have the innate, essential qualities of Balance, Shadowing, and Touch, without even one of which we could not live. Considering this, and considering that smell, hearing, and sight evolved as adjuncts to the primary senses, let us refer to them as the secondary senses.

Smell

Wigwam life here on the forested Mother's bosom gives me a feeling of aliveness that my urban years didn't know. When I enter my Lodge, I'm greeted by the mixed essences of Cedar bough bedding, smoked hides, the Raccoon oil my mittens were just treated with, and whatever foods and herbs are being cooked or dried. Tainting this potpourri is the faint odor of Skunk—the last meal of the Owl who gifted his skin to reside outstretched over my sleeping platform to bring Vision to dreamtime.

The smell of my Cedar bowl and spoon takes me back to the New Jersey Pine Barrens every time I use it. The smells in the air help me to forecast the weather, to track Deer and Porcupine (see the Sacred Hunt chapter of Book III). In any season, the Forest is ever alive with smells that involve me in a running dialogue on what is going on about me.

As musky beings ourselves, body scent, a primary part of body language, is important to our personal and social well being. Our scent changes with our emotional state; we are sexually aroused by body scents; women can tell the sex of a person by the smell of that person's breath. Many Old Way People don't feel comfortable talking to others unless they are close enough to smell them.

Civilized People carry their commitment to homogeneity over to the way they smell also. By masking and neutralizing their individual scents, they stress themselves and frustrate others in their efforts to communicate. Treating their physical environments similarly, only a small percentage of their sensory input comes through smell.

Even considering this, familiar smells evoke deeper and more lucid memories and emotions than do much more common and familiar sights and sounds. We've all no doubt noticed how a particular odor can very powerfully bring back the experience associated with that odor. In fact, were it not for the odor, we may not have even remembered the experience. Our odor (and related taste) memory is so strong because, in an evolutionary sense, it has been with us much longer than sight or hearing.

Smell is still naturally important to Civilized children until around adolescence, when they tend to reach a threshold of socialization. My daughter, whose first years were spent in the Civilized Way, found comfort in sleeping with her mother's shirt because it smelled like her. Children react strongly when their security blankets and stuffed animals are washed, because their parents have unwittingly eliminated the familiar, comforting smell.

Smell Exercises

In order to know the full range of smell's Gifts, we of the Civilized Way must overcome a tremendous amount of societal pressure to the contrary. We might begin by reading the Da'i chapter in Book III, which will help guide us to an understanding of personal hygiene stripped of its cultural baggage. As you read the chapter, it will become apparent to you that the practice of Da'i is essential to our sense of smell returning to enrich our lives. So the following exercises will be most gifting after we have begun Da'i.

Practice these exercises in the order presented, incorporating one into your living ritual before progressing to the next. The cumulative effect of these exercises done in sequence brings a depth of olfactory attunement that is seldom reached by selecting them randomly. Be mindful that our goal is not the completion of these exercises, but the joining with those of the Old Way in the awareness of the ever-turning Circle that attunement brings.

— Lift your bowl/plate to your nose and take time to lavish on the various smells before beginning to eat. (Our sense of smell is ten thousand times more acute than that of taste.)

— Open your house/car windows as much as possible, taking note of the changing smells you encounter and what they say to you. (When I begin such an exercise, I hang a note in a conspicuous place to remind me to practice it.)

— Part the ground cover and smell The Earth in a variety of areas, accounting for what may be causing the differences in smell. (Hint: To enliven the smell of something that is dry, first breathe on/through it.)

— Stick your nose in every blossom you encounter, noting the differences in scents as they relate to each type of flower, and the scents as they change in relation to temperature, humidity, age, and time of day.

— Smell your hair, and the hair and scalp of those close to you.

— Note how the smell of your underarms changes when you are fearful or angry as opposed to during physical exertion.

— Note how the smell of your scat changes with your diet and general health. (More on this subject in the Healing chapter of Book III.)

— Smell the genitals of your sexual partner and note if/how their scent affects you differently than before you began these exercises.

Hearing

Emulating one of my Guides, I strapped myself into the crotch of a low, scraggly Oak overhanging a granite bluff, which faced the oncoming summer Storm. Then I blindfolded myself and excitedly awaited my immersion in the far-rumbling Thunder.

The sentinel Wind hit with such force that I grabbed the Tree in panic. I feared the Tree and I were falling but had no way of knowing. Plastered against the Tree, I couldn't feel the earthpull. With treetops above, below, and on all sides, the hiss and moan that is usually overhead engulfed me, further adding to my disorientation. I couldn't visually confirm or deny what I was feeling. An adrenal rush born of fear of blindness supersensitized me. As a flash of lightning penetrated my bandana and eyelids, I impulsively jerked my head around to find its source and tell which way was up.

Overcome by uncontrollable rage, I tore the blindfold from my face, unstrapped myself, and hulked under the tree as big, gasping sobs of release overtook me. Within the space of a breath, it was over, and in again as much time I resolved never again to be the victim of my youthful but wisdom-shy enthusiasm.

Civilized Folks are sight-oriented; hearing accounts for only about ten percent of their sensory input. Even when they are receiving audio input, they use affirmations such as, "I see," and "It looks that way."

We retain only about a third of what we see: If we hear it as well, we retain twice as much. Sight and hearing work so well in unison because, evolving from the same nerve, they are closely related. (Some animals are thought to hear extremely low-frequency sounds with their eyes.)

Hearing has reached an impressive state of innate attunement with some of our fellow beings. I'm most enchanted by that of Owl, who can hunt solely by hearing. She can determine the direction of a sound source, just as we can, and she can simultaneously determine its elevation, which we cannot do. One of her ears is higher than the other, so the squeak of a Mouse in the grass below will reach her lower before her upper ear. The time difference between the reception of each ear gives her mouse's precise location below her.

Hearing Exercises

In the Civilized Way, hearing is needed only in crude form, whereas in the Old Way, as with Owl, a finely attuned sense of hearing is essential to Walking in Balance. Hearing attunement is easy for most People; just practice the following exercises (sequence unimportant) until new hearing patterns are established.

— Talk less, listen more. Talking keeps us in a rational-linear state of consciousness, discouraging rapport with the deeper mind. When we talk, we are basically repeating that which we already know; when we listen, we learn. And we must listen to remain attuned to the Greater Circle.

— Read less, listen more. We retain only about one-tenth of what we read; we retain twice as much of what we hear. (An unabridged recorded version of this book is available.) The bulk of Civilized words (whether written or spoken) are extraneous—space fillers. Fictional material exists largely as a substitute for what the Civilized Way does not allow its People to experience, and much non-fiction (this book included) is the Civilized Way's attempted compensation for its dearth of Elders and Guides.

Old Way Peoples do not have written forms to their languages because they do not need them. In fact, when presented by well-meaning colonizers, writing is usually rejected as an unnecessary and inadequate form of communication. The People have their history in their oral traditions, their teachers and inspiration in their legends and Elders, their romance and adventure in the lives they lead.

Yet even within the context of the Civilized Way, we can bring the gifts of hearing back to some of our communication. When possible, phone rather than write, and stand before each other for sharings of heart and spirit. Many books have recorded versions; check with your local library for availability.

— Owl stalk: Blindfold yourself. You'll hear better than with just your eyes closed, because you've erased even the possibility of seeing from your consciousness. Then spin to disorient yourself as your partner climbs a nearby tree (or stairs). Have him make rustling sounds just loud enough for you to detect, then you will point to him to check your accuracy. To determine your partner's angle of elevation, tilt your head to the side so that, like Owl's, one ear is higher than the other. (The similar blindfold stalking exercise in the Sacred Hunt chapter of Book II is another good hearing attuner.)

— Circle Hearing: The civilized tendency is to key in on one sound, one voice, one Birdsong, and tune out the rest of the lifechorus. As an instrumental solo sounds better within the context of its band, so do other voices when embellished by the chorus of their kin. It is also the Native Way to keep attuned to the entire Circle while focused on a particular thing. (We've discussed the reasons for this in earlier chapters.) We automatically practice Circle hearing upon Coming to Oneness.

Suggestions to improve your hearing and accuracy: The wind carries sounds with it, so a wind from the right will make a sound's source appear to be more to the left, and a tailwind will give the illusion of the source being further away. Rising air thermals distort sound, making its source seem further away and lower. Damp air carries sound well, bringing its source deceptively closer. At night, because of the quiet, and because night air is usually more humid and still than day air, sound sources seem closer and can be more accurately pinpointed. Magnify sounds by placing your thumbs behind your ears, cupping your hands to create larger ears and pointing them toward the sound source. Open your mouth a bit to better hear low frequency sounds.

Sight

Sun was leaving me in favor of His night's journey below the trees. His departure was quickened by an incoming blanket of low, mushy clouds that often covers us late in the Falling Leaves Moon. I was gathering Sweetfern and the last of the Ground-cherries out on the Prairie, trying to do more than I was given time for, as was my custom when I was young.

Already having pushed much after light would allow, I gave my Song of Thanksgiving and rose to a thick, soggy-aired night. I had no trail to follow and a mile of thick, variegated Forest, Bog, and granite outcrop to traverse. This is the first time I was forced to reach camp in dark this dense, and also the first chance to put my night vision training to practice, so I was as keyed as a Weasel on a last-chance stalk.

So I would have the aid of my primal senses, I meditated to Come to Oneness and then took a short time longer to attune myself to the voice of my deeper brain.

Even in this murky night, some residual Starshine filtered through, but once in the Forest, it did little more than identify the occasional breaks in the dense canopy. My feet became as eyes, feeling each step before I committed to it. I traveled slowly, allowing my infant unseen eyes the time to sense the spirit-side (aura) of trees and rocks whose physical side I could not see. My innate sense of direction kept me on course.

A sense of timelessness pervaded my trek, as I was, of necessity, very intimately absorbed in the now. It took roughly two hours to walk that mile, and I came to within twenty paces of the trailbase to my ridgetop Wigwam.

That experience had such a deep effect on me that my recounting it is as though I were reliving it. The intense involvement I had to muster to force my lazy, untrained Civilized eyes to see left me drained and sweat-soaked. I was hit with the impact of how little of what I looked at I actually saw, especially in such a complex environment and under such unusual conditions. And I was given the awareness that the Air, although transparent, has living energies within its expanse that can also be seen. In other words, sight starts at my iris, rather than at the first solid object beyond.

Sight Exercises

First, let us become aware of how we can treat our eyes with respect, so that they are capable of the vision we seek:

— Read less, and for shorter periods of time. Avoid fine print.

— Use artificial lighting, particularly flourescent, only when necessary.

— Keep midday Sun from shining directly in eyes.

At the same time, let us leave binoculars and similar apparatus behind, as they are crutches that keep us lazy and isolated. With them we have little incentive to develop the attunement and immersion skills that would bring us close enough so as not to need binoculars, as well as to use our other senses in conjunction with sight. It is the difference between watching from a hilltop while others swim, and going down to swim with them.

The simplest way to better observation is to keep eyes open, both literally and figuratively. In the Old Way, the Guardian is ever observant, ever alert, even during meditation and sleep. The Visionary can see through awaketime to dreamtime, and vice-versa. The Book II Dreams chapter covers methods for integrating dream and awake times: the following exercise brings instant sight-recognition, and eventually conscious awareness, to our sleeptime.

Conscious Sleep (A Sight Exercise)

It is possible to be aware of our surroundings while sleeping, and still be fully absorbed in dreamtime. Very few are naturals at this; most of us will need a long and increasingly intensive training period. It requires a partner who is able to periodically wake and quiz us. The object is, upon being awoken, to quickly give time of night, location in which we are sleeping, direction we are facing, and eventually, what sounds or disturbances occurred, and when, since we were last awoken.

Switch your sleeping location each night, from upstairs, to downstairs, to the couch, to the floor, etc., and alter the direction in which you sleep. When in your bed, turn it or sleep in it the opposite way.

Have your partner wake you just once or twice a night until the speed and accuracy of your response begins increasing. Then keep adding an awakening per night as you improve, until you reach about five per night. Vary the number each night, using five as an average, and space the awakenings randomly, so they do not give you a clue as to the time.

Gauge your progress on how easily you awake, how quickly you become cognizant, and how easily you fall back to sleep. As your sensitivity increases, have your partner wake you in more and more subtle ways, perhaps by shuffling his feet as he enters or by breathing loudly. The epitome of this exercise is to be able to sense your partner's presence and awake without him making a sound. As unattainable as this level of awareness may seem, it is possible for each of us.

I prepare for Conscious Sleep by taking some time to acquaint myself with my surroundings before going to bed, particularly if I'm in a new place. When visiting friends in the city, I tour the house to become familiar with its layout and decor, and my sleeping place in relation to it. Then, just before turning in, I walk the neighborhood to know the house's (and my) place in its greater Circle.

Once in bed, I befriend my immediate surroundings so that I'll be comfortable and familiar with their appearance and sounds and smells. Then I close my eyes and touch their spirits as I enter Dreamtime.

To both practice and facilitate this exercise at the same time is not possible. If your partner also wants to develop conscious sleep, have one of you guide the other through the entire process before switching roles.

The exercises to follow are designed to develop the full dimension of sight:

Sweeping Sight

Sweeping Sight and Circle Sight (which follows) are skills closely associated with the Hunt (see sister volume), although they have a much broader application. Sweeping Sight intensively covers a broad area with focused sight, while Circle Sight is panoramic. Sweeping Sight is used specifically in situations where we do not know the general location of our quarry and can stand still to mount a directed visual search; Circle Sight is used at all other times.

Begin Sweeping Sight by choosing a position for yourself that gives a broad, uninterrupted view of the area to be searched. Stalk into position if you wish to remain unannounced (stalking is covered in Sacred Hunt chapter of Book III). An area as wide as a third of a circle is the maximum that can be sweep sighted.

Then, with focused sight, sweep slowly back and forth (eyes move horizontally much easier than vertically) across the search area, beginning at your feet and working outward to the area's horizon. Keep your line of search narrow so that you don't miss anything, and study any movement, changes in form, texture, color, and lines that run at angles contrary to their background. Also note shadows that may give the location of something well camouflaged, and keep alert to telltale concentric rings.

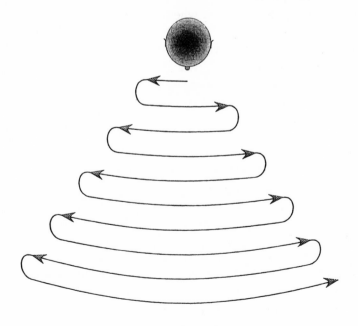

Chart 10. Sweeping Sight

Owl, my Dodem, showed me a way to make Sweeping Sight more effective. As I watched her Sweep, she raised and lowered her head and moved it to the right and left. This gave her a number of angles of perception, and thereby less chance of missing something. (Bear scans similarly, swinging his head from right to left while walking.) I use this technique in particular when something catches my eye and I want to study it further.

Circle Sight

Unlike Sweeping Sight, we do not focus or pattern search when using Circle Sight. We take in the full panorama of our field of vision, remaining sensitive to any oddity that catches the eye. We focus only to further study something, as in Sweeping Sight, then switch back to Circle Sight.

I used to get so absorbed in what I was observing that I'd forget to return to Circle Sight. One early Green Season dusk I was watching a Deer cautiously grazing at Woods' edge and only by chance eventually noticed her Fawn lingering in the shadows. Worse yet, I missed a pair of yearlings, in full sight barely a stone's throw away from mother and offspring.

We use Circle Sight at all times when we are moving, and when we are stationary but not searching. It works well when covering a lot of territory to identify likely areas for the more thorough and time-consuming Sweeping Sight.

Most sight-oriented animals, whether prey or predator, rely primarily on Circle Sight. Small prey animals use it almost exclusively, even when fleeing, whereas chasing predators switch to focused sight. Some predators specialize in specific types of Circle Sight (as do Hawks with movement, and Ferrets with shadow), and many prey have bulging eyes positioned on the sides of their heads so that their field of vision is nearly the entire circumference.

Circle Sight is also used to keep attuned to the Greater Circle when occupied with something that doesn't demand eye involvement. Being accustomed to eye contact, I was initially unnerved by the first Wolves and Native People I talked with; even though they were fully involved in our discussion, their sight went beyond me. I felt that I did not have their undivided attention, and, in fact, I didn't. They remained attuned to the ever-changing Circle. Those of the Old Way exist within the flow of everything about them, and everything exists within them.

When I leave a familiar area without noticing something new, or when I get involved in a discussion or activity to the point that I miss something going on in my Circle, I feel that I have failed my training and possibly deprived myself of an experience or awareness that was intended for me. For a Guardian, the cost is steeper, as he could be putting others at risk.

Memory Sight

We've all heard that a picture is worth a thousand words; this bit of folk wisdom also applies to mental pictures. We all have what is commonly referred to as photographic memory, which is innate and functional in each of us to a varying degree. This power of visual recall is so commonly used, and so easily strengthened, that the rewards (which range from no longer misplacing keys to being able to reflect on the nuances of color in last night's Sunset), are more than worth the practice of these simple exercises:

— Immediately after leaving a familiar place, recall its image and note at least one thing that you hadn't seen before. Do the same after concluding an absorbing discussion or activity.

— With a partner, visit a place unfamiliar to you. View your surroundings, using Circle Sight, and don't make an effort to consciously memorize what you see. Meet at a later time, close your eyes for a dozen breaths to recall the place's image, then quiz each other on what you've seen.

— To perform amazing feats like locating misplaced keys, first Come to Oneness (see Circle Attunement chapter), then visualize the path of your steps when you lost your keys, and you may see them. Some become easily discouraged with this exercise, because there's no gauge of progress—either it works or it doesn't. Practice usually brings greater success, but if in time it doesn't, it is likely because of the clutter and overload in one's life. If that be the case, I would like to share a suggestion from Henry David Thoreau that worked for me—"Simplify, simplify, simplify."

— Have your partner lay a couple dozen small, varied items out for you to observe for a short period of time (six breaths is a good starting point), then cover them. Now list everything you can recall, being specific as to color, size, texture, the location of each and what it was next to. Adjust observation time to ability, and as you improve, wait for longer periods of time before doing the recall. I like to conduct this exercise impromptu in the Woods, quickly gathering a variety of items, arranging them in front of me, then having participants turn their backs and record what they've seen. A second look to verify notes and check what was missed helps to sharpen the skill.

Spirit Sight

In the life-experience introducing this section on Sight, I mentioned seeing the spirit-side of things. Because spirit is half of everything, seeing spirit is the only way we can fully see. In the Old Way, Spirit Sight is intrinsic to lifeway, whereas Civilized Beings perpetually stumble in their judgements because they are based on half-sight. Deceivers wear thin cover when their spirits are naked to others.

For all but a blessed few, Spirit Sight is extremely near-sighted. Most of us need to be close enough to touch something in order to see its spirit. Guiding others to see Spirit from a distance goes well beyond the scope of this book, but I can tell you that, just as for Native People, lack of this ability need not be an impediment. In the Old Way, there is trust in those who are far-sighted in a spirit way; we also, once we know the Old Way, can trust in its Seers.

I have yet to meet a high-strung or highly stressed person (Human or otherwise) who can Spirit See. If this might include you, it is my prayer that after we walk our Journey together in this series of books, you will be able to come back to this step and find your Spirit Sight.

Most of us are presently capable of very near-sighted Spirit Sight. We can begin by choosing an area of large-treed Forest, a field of boulders, or whatever our area has to offer that would have a great presence of spirit. To minimize interference, find a quiet area away from power lines. Then Come to Oneness and have your partner blindfold you and give you a couple turns. (Your partner assists so that you do not risk dulling the sharp edge of Oneness with concern over readying yourself.)

Now rub your hands vigorously together, extend them comfortably in front of you with palms out, and begin everso-slowly walking forward. As you approach an object, your sensitized hands will feel its form before you touch it.

Initially you may be almost touching an object before you detect it, and you may well touch many without first detecting them at all. Atrophied Spirit Sight is very difficult to resuscitate, so I encourage you to persist, as you will eventually show progress. Your hands are the unseen eyes of your primary senses; as those senses strengthen, so will your Spirit Sight.

As you do progress, you will notice that you are sensing spirit farther and farther away from its physical form. This will continue to a distance (which varies with each individual) beyond which you will not be able to extend. As you further progress, you will no longer need your hands, and you will begin to see spirit with your eyes open.

Because of the state of high tension and energy drain, ten minutes at a time is long enough for this exercise. Fatigue and inefficiency set in if tried any longer.

Night Vision

More than half of our non-Human kin are nocturnal; we miss a lot by not knowing the night. But many of us feel that we cannot see at night, or that we have poor night vision. In comparison to some night dwellers, such as Cat, whose eye takes in ten times more light than ours, our Night Vision is weak. Others have abandoned light-based sight and instead have found extremely efficient use of sound, heat, smell, and touch. Still, we can see quite well at night, even when compared with many nocturnal animals. And our nocturnal visual abilities can be augmented by relying more on senses other than sight, as many other animals do.

That the night is dark is a misconception many inside dwellers hold to. We look into the night from a lighter place (including cars and cities), so our eyes are not focused to utilize the sparser night light. Even if we were to step out of the light, our iris's muscles (out of condition from little use) would have trouble fine-tuning our pupils to the night light.

The light comes from Moonshine and Starshine, half of which is available even through clouds. In the Green Season, we have the afterglow of Sun, which is not far below the Northern horizon; in the White Season, we are blessed with the reflective glow of Snow, which magnifies available light and provides a light background against which things can be more easily seen. Many other surfaces reflect and magnify light, such as sand and leaves. Woodland trails and bordering tree trunks, often indiscernible in the dark, can sometimes be located by studying the lay of the leaves.

Our Night Vision is black and white because the retina's cones, which are color sensitive, only work in daylight. Even if we had color vision, many colorful animals would still appear black and white. For example, birds with brightly colored or iridescent plumage often don't appear to be so because of feather pigment, but because the feather structure acts as a prism to refract Sunlight and reflect back only certain colors of the spectrum. This is the case with Bluejay, a member of the Crow-Raven family, who is also black when viewed at night by flashlight or in firelight.

Just as we have done with day sight, we can relearn how to see at night. Twilight is a good time to greet the night, as our eyes will then have time to naturally adjust to the waning light. If it is already nightfall, open your eyes wide, which stimulates pupil adjustment. When leaving the fireside or a lighted room, close one eye a few minutes in advance of leaving. You'll then have one eye already adjusted to the dark, giving you a quick and stumble-free transition.

For me (and you also?), great childhood examples of adjustment to twilight are the times when I was expected home before dark and was greeted by parents who insisted against my protests that it was already dark. From their well-lit indoor vantage point, I can now understand how it definitely looked dark to them, even though I, attuned to the twilight, could still see quite well.

Here are a few hints for more efficient Night Vision:

— When you lose sight of something, look off to the side of it and it will often reappear.

— When you need to focus or detect movement, limit your field of vision by cupping a hand around the outside of each eye to create side-blinders.

— Unless you're watching for silhouettes, keep a dim light source, such as Moon, twilight, or firelight, behind you.

When Native Peoples need portable light, they use one that is dim and diffused, so that it covers a wide area and augments, rather than overpowers the natural light. One can still see beyond the light's range, as it is not so bright that it interferes with Night Sight. A version of a Native lantern can be easily made from a three pound coffee can: Set the can upright and punch a hole midway up the side to hold a regular table-size candle. On the opposide side, punch holes to affix a hoop handle (coathanger wire works well). To use, insert a candle so that its lit end is inside the can and can be pushed up as it burns down. The open top will project a beam in the direction pointed. This candle lantern is windproof and can be tossed in the air without going out.

Our Senses in Old Way Perspective

A particular sense does not exist outside the context of the other senses. In fact, the dividing lines we have here constructed between the senses are rather artificial, done only so that we could more easily Walk this Path toward sensory attunement. We are one sensory organ, a being of one marvelously multi-talented sense with one grand purpose—to maintain attunement with The Balance. The following recounting is an illustration of this awareness, as no particular "sense" can be credited with my performance. The story also shows how sensory attunement can reflect in all that we do, including that at which we are not practiced.

When my Wigwam was five days' paddle east of here, I had a friend living a mile north across the Swamp who was a marksman and gun collector. We respected each other's approaches to the Hunt, while at the same time enjoying the banter we threw back and forth concerning their relative merits and demerits. (If it weren't for his accident-crippled limbs, I was convinced my friend would be cradling a bow instead of a bullet-belcher.)

For years he tried to entice me to shoot a gun, and for years I'd reply with some jibing remark. Then, one sub-zero night in the Big Snow Moon, I conceded. I stopped in for some tea and fireside banter and found him in the woodshop setting up a pistol target—a magazine-page figure tacked to a chunk of firewood set on end at the far corner of the building.

My first bullet took the paper figure's breast pocket deep into the log behind him, but my second one left no trace. Was it a blank or was I so far off that it went through the wall someplace? Finally my friend checked in what he considered the unlikeliest place; he split the log and found the second bullet smashed into the back of the first one.

That was the first (and last) time I had shot a gun in thirty years.

Envisioning

This chapter's exercises are substitutes for growing up in the Old Way, as life for Native People is a continuous exercise in sensory attunement. However, Envisioning is one unique exercise and potent form of guidance they do practice in their quest for attunement.

It is not always necessary to walk through a situation in order to experience it; we can often do the same thing internally, involving the same sensual experiences, with this technique. Not being limited by physical constraints, it opens us to a whole new range of experiences.

Again, Coming to Oneness is the first step. Then create the setting in your mind's eye, add the props, and have your experience.

Envisioning works to some degree in honing sensory skills but works better in using already developed skills to explore possibilities or run scenarios. For instance, when exploring new territory, I like to envision campsite possibilities, enacting the range of considerations from food and firewood availability to storm shelter and environmental impact. This way, I'm learning even when I can't be physically involved, and I'm covering considerably more territory than would be physically possible.

When Envisioning a scenario, we are empowering it to happen. If we envision a full range of scenarios, we greatly reduce the risk of causing one to unfold that may not be the best choice.

Ridicule

In Old Way cultures, constructive Ridicule is a commonly accepted method of expression and guidance. Used ritually and respectfully, most anything is fair game (see references to Contraries in index). Within the guidelines of custom, it is available to every age, gender, and title as a spontaneous and straightforward social tool.

Often emotionally charged and demeaningly delivered, Civilized Ridicule becomes a negative, ego-bruising experience. To Native People, it is a finely honed and evolved instructional tool—a respectfully given and welcomed form of guidance. That an Elder or Guide would take the time to address one's weaknesses or shortcomings is considered a personal Honor, a sign of worthiness, and the recipient gives thanks for the guidance. However, if resentment is shown, a Guide will save his words for those with a thirst for wisdom and a pride that walks in humility.

I used to think the Woods is a place to get away from it all and experience peace and solitude. Ads and movies, friends, books, and teachers—they all told me to seek the farther places.

But quiet and isolation was hardly what I wanted—that's what I was suffering from there amidst the hum and bustle. I was immersed in movement and activity, but I didn't feel life. I was a young adult, fighting to stay out of a war I couldn't understand and struggling against the vacuum of the omnipresent glitter that drew me away from the Woods of my youth.

One early morning I stormed out of the City in a fit of frustration. After I had gone some distance, an old mossy Log asked me to sit down upon him and join him in greeting the Dawn. The last of Dark Season's blanket had just been rolled back, and Sun was working hard to warm the sodden Earth.

Then something entered and overcame me that tingled and enlivened my senses. In the "quiet" Forest, I was inundated by explosions of sap-bloated buds above me, raucous unfurlings of tender, emerging herbs at my feet, and gushing new freshets of the juices of life all about me. Sky shouted a blue so damp and pregnant that his very breathing gave the elixir of new life to old.

I couldn't return to the arsenic din; from then on my Song of Being found resonance in the place where life screams through the Silence.

Mental Attunement

I blow into the jaws of the Skullflute, sparking a thin, sharp music that gains timbre and volume as it reverberates in the expansive backskull. The breath comes from me, yet when it comes back upon me it sings of the self I chance upon only occasionally in the deep reaches of a Sacred Dream.

My hands, cradling both my lower jaw and that of the Flute, carry the resonance into my head. I look into the hollow eyes of the Skull and feel as though I am, at the same time, the Skull looking back into me. We are twirling, the Flute and I, on perspectives of the same sharing that are too close to be those of lovers.

My skull is covered with olive skin and grizzled hair; the Skullflute is of a deep ivory color with moss green dapples and is glazed, having much the appearance of porcelainware. He is airy, fragile. His fine-lined jaws protrude Apelike, and his sloping forehead meets a rising backskull that is broad and deep and two or three times the volume of mine.

Along his lower jaw are the fingerholes I play, or more accurately, am guided to play. The fingers are mine in name, yet their melodious dance is drawn forth by the Skull and directed by the forces too far within and beyond for me to know. Lost to a timeless trance, we play and play until we breathe ourselves entirely into each other and again resonate the Song of the Ancestors.

Rational intelligence is the god of the Civilized; they worship the bulging brain. If The Great Mother could only have found a way to walk with this new god, perhaps we would not have been barred from Balance (the biblical Eden). As it is, the Way of The Mother exists in realms not only alien to, but defying, rational comprehension. So when plagued by the inevitable vicissitudes of imbalance and eluded by the peace of the Circle, the Civilized are handicapped—they know only to turn to the sacred frontal bulge upon which they have been conditioned to rely.

Without the perceptivity, insight, and sensory grounding borne of synchronous function with the primal brain, the rational brain addresses life with all the depth and sensitivity of a computer viewing a sunset. Thus the Civilized approach to life is as we would expect from a computer—pragmatic and quantified.

Using the rational brain as the doorway to life is like looking through a keyhole when one could throw open the door and enter. The keyhole view is rationally digestible; it has defined boundaries and limited dimension. Beyond the door is boundless immersion. Boundlessness defies boundary and immersion defies dimension, giving the rational mind nothing to bite and chew.

For Native People there is little question about opening that door and stepping through. In fact, it is not a choice as Civilized People would know it. As Cricket has one "choice" of lovesong if he wishes a mate, a Native "chooses" the Lifedance if she desires Balance.

We have three distinct brains, of which our nervous system is an extension. Sensory organs are no more than modified nerve endings. Our various brains evolved to refine specific brain functions in serving the senses, just as our specific senses evolved to serve and refine intuition.

Our Old Brain is little more than a bulge in the spinal cord. We were gifted it by our far distant Ancestors—the simplest of animals with spinal cords, and we share it in kinship with nearly all spinal-corded non-Human People. It is the center of Balance and the regulator of unconscious acts such as digestion and circulation.

The secondary senses, along with emotions and the urge to mate, are handled by our Mid Brain, which we received from our fish, amphibian, and reptilian Ancestors. Both our Old and Mid Brains are little changed from those of our long-ago Ancestors.

Within our New Brain is the ability to imagine, reason, hold conscious memory—and control/modify our other brains.

This control potential, this innate glitch that allows the distortion of mental function, is the method by which Civilization achieves socio-politico-religious conformity. In fact, this squelching of the older brains must be demanded of the Civilized in order to secure their Way's survival and dominance. (By school age, most children are mentally out of Balance. Those retaining some vestigial Balance usually succumb after entering school, as the schools are Civilization's major proponent of New Brain dominance.)

Specifically, the New Brain's abilities to sequentialize time and conform matter are the pillars of the Civilized Way. This uniquely radical and species-specific concept of perception leads the Civilized People to hold the New Brain as the epitome of Creation—an adaptive advantage over their other life-kin. Perhaps Civilization is a grand-scale New Brain experiment to see where a lifeway based on time and matter will take its adherents.

From the perspective of the Circle, every brain is a gift of Creation and a glory to behold—the epitome of its kind. Ours is only one of many options. Only when our three brains function in symphony do we function within the realm of Balance for our Kind. Then we function from our true center, our Heart-of-Hearts.

Civilized Humans, not knowing their Heart-of-Hearts, are not capable of Circle perspective. To the great misfortune of the Life-Circle, they cannot know that their advantage is illusory, that their perceived competitive edge is in actuality the teetering edge of a precipice. If the Civilized Way persists, the epitaph of our species may well read that we were a scant, finite, and expendible microcosm of the Circle of Life.

The New Brain has two sides, each with a distinct mode of thinking. One, already briefly mentioned, is characteristic of Civilized People and in them usually predominates over the other. Let's refer to it as the linear side. The other side, which we'll call the spatial side, functions in Balance with the linear side in Native People.

In men, the connection between the two sides of the New Brain usually erodes away with puberty, so they have to work at maintaining mental clarity and Balance (one reason the Sweat Lodge and Vision Quest are more needed by men). Women demonstrate their retained connection by integrated perspective, natural ease at nurturing, and strong, innate relationship with The Earth Mother. Creative men are often spatial brainside dominant, indicated by their tendency toward left-handedness. (The spatial side largely controls the left side of the body.)

The following chart more clearly illustrates these sometimes opposing and sometimes complementary modes of thinking:

Linear Side	Spatial Side
learn by rote	learn by discovery
think in words	think in symbols
write in nouns	write in verbs
expressive	expresses in images
words used to signal	words used to design
speed thinking	contemplative thinking
sequential thinking/memory	image thinking/memory
how things work; cause	what works; result
analytic ability	perceptive ability
categorizing, dissective	assembling, holistic
time conscious	flow conscious
fact conscious	feeling conscious
form conscious	spirit conscious
guidance by rationale, ideal	guidance by Dream, Vision

I don't wish that we leave this chapter with the impression that the spatial side of the brain is superior to the linear side. Everything we are given is for an honorable purpose; only by misusing our Gifts do we show disrespect to Creation. When not subjugating her twin side and when in Balance with her older sibling brains, the linear side is essential to the attunement we seek.

And I do not wish those of us who find ourselves in the Civilized Way to end this chapter despairing. We are intended to walk the Old Way in mental attunement; it is so intrinsic to our makeup that once we begin taking conscious steps, a momentum gains within us that empowers our Journey homeward.

Mental Exercises

Because of its nature, much of our Journey together is exercises in mental attunement.

Our midbrain, being the receiving, synthesizing, and storage point for external stimuli, becomes attuned as we attune our senses and choose our Circle. When we forego habitual actions and responses and begin to function from our Heart-of-Hearts, we start using those parts of the midbrain that have been in long hibernation for lack of something to do. This exercise prepares us to respond to unique and unpredictable situations.

Repetitive, habitual, and trained behaviors—the great bulk of Civilized functioning—rely over and over upon the same small part of the brain. This is true also of the rational processes, which involve perhaps three to five percent of the brain. I've heard people express concern over losing touch with themselves if they were to quiet their rational-habitual selves. To the contrary, they could be opening themselves to vast reaches of their mindscapes that have been so squelched by the tiny, analytical robot-brain.

Perhaps Civilization is a grand-scale New Brain experiment to see where a lifeway based on time and matter will take its adherents.

The Forest is my Cathedral — the moss is its floor,
the branches overhead are its roof, the spire of Elder Pine is its steeple . . .
its choral voice is the gift of bird and Wind, its altar is the vision of Sun and Moon . . .

Spiritual Attunement

"Spiritual experience, as I see it in this day, is primarily emotionalism. Those who are not accustomed to living their spirituality may consider a service or ceremony to be their spiritual experience; they may consider the feeling derived from such an experience to be a spiritual feeling.

They are a spiritual people who breathe and walk their Spirituality; ceremony is quite a different experience for them than for those whose spirituality is wrapped up and delivered like pizza. On the Path of our Ancestors, spirit walks within each person so that one can't be told from the other. There is no experience, no Dream on that Path, that is not to both spirit and flesh as though they were one."

—She Who Talks With Loons

"For the whole life-effect of man is to get in direct contact with the elemental life of the cosmos, mountain-life, cloud-life, thunder-life, air-life, earth-life, sun-life. To come into immediate felt contact, and so derive energy, power, and a sort of deep joy. This effort into sheer naked contact, without an intermediary or mediator, is the real meaning of religion."

—D.H. Lawrence

Religion and Spirituality

Religion serves a generic god who speaks a universal message; Spirituality serves the individual, whose god speaks to him. The practice of Religion is the following of set rules and guidelines in approaching god; the practice of Spirituality is a search for the Spirit Within and its harmony with the Spirit Without. Religious life is imposed by the supernatural; Spiritual life blossoms in the unfolding of the natural life.

Spiritual People don't worship their god, as that would necessitate a separation from their god. They are of their god and their god is of them. Religious People know two worlds; their god often exists in the *other* one.

Religion is a surviving remnant of another time—a sanctification and oftentimes rote perpetuation of self-sanctified ritual and belief; Spirituality is the living Voice of the Ancestors, the guiding wisdom of Elders, and the Song and Vision of each individual.

Religion tends to be a duality of eternal opposites—god and antigod, good and evil, life and death, here and hereafter, body and spirit, truth and untruth, past and future, right and wrong, Eden and banishment. And amongst Religionists is the prolific duality of opinion resulting from endless debates amongst its countless sub-religions.

Spirituality is Oneness; there is no this way or that way. God is flesh *and* spirit, Eden was Earth and is Earth. Spiritualists are aware that spirit dwells in all things and knows neither word nor direction, time nor conscience nor purpose. Anything beyond that to the Spiritualist is a Human attempt to create spirit, corner it, and use it to some end.

Religion usually has Leaders; its hierarchy and resultant bureaucratism spawn a dogmatism that is presented as "The Way" to their masses, while at the same time preserving certain inner sanctum teachings for the elite. Inevitably, an elitist attitude forms that exempts them from the creed of the followers.

Religion can be taught apart from life; Spirituality is lived and thus becomes known. The Spirit-Way has Guides, who direct those who come to them away from them in order that Seekers may find their own connection with spirit, their personal place of Power and Balance, their Medicine-Way. They are then guided to gift the Blessings of their Way for the enrichment of their People.

The term "Spiritual Leader" can be viewed as an oxymoron—a contradiction within itself. In walking one's Path, one does not, can not, live another. A leader, by the very act of leading, denies the spirituality of those who follow. We each have a personal Vison, either already received or yet awaiting, and we each have a Path to walk the Vision that is unique to us. Those who follow deny the fullness of their Vision. In doing so, they refuse many of its blessings, both for themselves and others. Those who lead do the same, abandoning the unique angles in their Paths for the gentle curves palatable to others. In order for leader and follower to share, they adopt a common generic approach to spirituality, i.e. Religion. Spiritual Leaders do not exist; in actuality they are purveyors of Religion.

Because of conditioning to a given, structured approach to life, many of the Civilized Way are inherently drawn to Religious Leaders. What they sacrifice of their Personal Power is compensated for by the easy fulfillment of those deep longings that their culture has left empty. They often cannot see what they have bartered of themselves to buy this peace. And if they do see it, they may do it anyway. When one feels lonely, his innate urge to survive can smooth all protest.

Knowing well the pain and longing borne of isolation from spirit, I raise my Song from the depths of my being to empower this Journey-step so that we can risk the trust that brings trusting and the gifts that bring giving. We no longer walk alone; let us support each other in finding that unfettered place where spirit dwells.

In Religion there is little room for Vision (see Vision chapter in Book II), for direct personal contact with spirit. Attempting such would sidestep Religion's hierarchical approach to spirit, thus undermining Religion's reason for existence. The return to personal Vision could well deem Religion irrelevant.

Those of the Spirit-Way are fellow Seekers; those of the Religious Way are often followers of gurus and popes. They stress the connection with other People; those of Spirit seek the connection within and beyond the self. To them, there is no Human-directed way. Their Guides are merely inspirations, tool-givers. If they begin to teach, they found a Religion, and those who listen join it.

Spirituality became Religion when the embryonic Civilized Way dichotomized itself from the means and ends of its existence. This separateness became Civilization's self-serving doctrine of dualistic perspective— the primary tool in the justification and promotion of its ways. Already despiritualized for exploitation, The Mother Earth became associated with the "alien" and "sinful" Old Way. The "unsaved"—the "low class, poor, dirty, sick, drunken"—were created, labeled, and relegated to Her. Defrocked of physical aspect, the Sky Father was made pure spirit and crowned as the exclusive possession and omnipotent champion of Civilization. As such, He became the antithesis of The Mother. His "followers" were the "chosen ones," the "blessed," those destined to "inherit the earth."

This was a necessary move for budding Civilization; clearly separating the spiritual and material (i.e., church and state) gave the state autonomy in the physical realm and awarded Religion unchallenged control of the Spiritual realm. This pact divvied the spoils of Civilization in such a clean and mutually exclusive way that church and state could function in parallel without interfering with, or being answerable to, each other.

Often Spirituality's adaptation of Civilized organizational and controlling structures (necessary to its joining Civilization) allowed it, as Religion, to come back and control the very state that forced its isolation from the physical realm. A classic example is found in the transition of the Roman Empire to the Holy Roman Empire.

The Christian tradition holds a potent example of the rift between Spirituality and Religion. Many prophets and healers arose during Christianity's transitional time, attempting to preserve and restore its Mother aspect and some of its Old Way Beauties. These prophets had little lasting effect; as with all the Spiritual Paths that vied for Civilized favor, it had to be purged of its relevance to the physical.

In the first centuries of its organized existence, the Roman Church called its hierarchy to great councils to purge itself of surviving vestiges of the Old Way. One casualty was the second half of their best-known prayer (which is attributed to their namesake, when in actuality it existed long before). That half yet exists (along with much of the Beauty of the early Christian Way, in hidden archives that survived the purgings). The following is a rough translation:

> Our Mother, the Earth, honored are You by us. Your Kingdom come, your Way be followed by us, as by all that are of You. As you send every day your Blessings, send them also to us. Forgive us our harming You, as we atone for all the hurt we cause You. And lead us not into sickness, but deliver us from all imbalance, for You are the Earth, the Flesh, and the health. Amen.

Religion holds that there is a proper place to talk to its god. A religious person, in conveying this concept to a spiritual person, might get this reply, "The Forest is my Cathedral—the moss is its floor, the branches overhead are its roof, the spire of Elder Pine is its steeple. Its incense is the essence of pitch and blossom, its choral voice is the Gift of bird and Wind, its altar is the vision of Sun and Moon through stout branches." Neither of them is likely to be aware of how related their cathedrals really are . . .

Pre-Hellenic People sang their Honor and Thanksgiving under an embracing Circle of Elder Trees. With their massive, rooted trunks and canopy of stout sheltering branches, these timeless Ancients imparted a calming presence and engendering Power.

When these People left the Forest and the Hunt for the field and the plow, they brought their Forest temples with them. They planted their uprooted trees upside-down in Circles in the centers of their villages, so Ceremony could continue to be practiced in the familiar, reassuring presence of the Ancients. Now their roots, rather than their limbs formed the overhead canopy.

In time, as those things of Earth became a metaphor to evolving Civilization, the temple trunks were plastered over to more resemble the character of the structures about them. Later the trunks became pillars made entirely of stone. In simulation of their sylvan predecessors, they were of smaller diameter at the base and had fluted tops. And in compliance with Civilized form, they began to be arranged in linear fashion.

The next step was to enclose the space between the pillars to recapture the quiet of the Forest and to weatherproof the structure, creating an overhead dome of the fluted tops. Now the isolation from The Living Mother was complete. Yet the massive pillars and sheltering dome were prominent; the feeling of the Elders' presence survived.

Within the context of Western Civilization, the Medieval Cathedral, with its massive buttresses, high-vaulted ceilings, and stained glass windows simulating the dappled, filtered sunlight that reaches the Forest floor, is the epitome of the Civilized Human spirit's search for its lost sacred space. When I walk up its steeple-shadowed steps, open the massive Oak door, and step into the dim, high-ceilinged chamber with rainbow-tinged light streaming down from above and the smell of incense from rituals past lingering in the stone-chilled air, I'm taken by the same spirit-lifting sensation as when I stand beneath the Forest Ancients.

The Mosques of the Mideast, the Temples of India and the Far East, and Eastern Rite Churches all have the same spirit-awakening characteristics as do Medieval Cathedrals. However, the majority of the newly constructed houses of worship in the West are practical, low undomed affairs that give breath to my soul no more than does a gymnasium. Perhaps this is a reason for the decline of traditional Religion's power.

Along with the decline of traditional Religion, and somewhat anecdotal to it, is the rise of pop Spirituality—weekend workshops on becoming a Shaman, Drum-trance tapes, a few minutes of guided drumming to find one's Animal Guardian, mini-Vision Quests, wisdoms and ceremonies being marketed and sold. Participants may be initially impressed but soon find their experiences to be shallow and their inspirations to be short-lived. The flash carries little fire into their lives.

These attempted marriages of the Sacred with quick-fix, self-absorbed, and fast-lane consumerism are aberrations to many—a grand trivialization of the Spirit-Way. They do not work in part because they lose Power when taken out of their cultural context, and in part because there are no shortcuts—the Path must be walked in order to learn from its steps. The Healer who does not die does not know how to bring life; Vision not cried and fasted for is clouded, weak, and distorted. Guardians do not appear on cue. Buying one's way into a Path cheapens it and disgraces those who walk it in answer to a Calling, who are inspired and prepared to gift it their time, dedication, and lifeblood.

This trendy Spirituality has new gurus—spirits from other times or places who speak through people, speak in words, and give general guidance. Their messages are of higher intelligences, time and destiny, hierarchy, and usually a master plan of which they are the purveyors/ informants. This is all alien to the Old Way. Stepping back into Greater Circle Perspective bares this phenomenon's actual identity—warmed-over Religion.

There is no word for Religion in the languages of Native People. Just as the fiery colors of the Autumn Forest do not exist apart from it, so is Religion nonexistent as a distinct concept with Native People. It is said that they live their Religion, but more accurately, they *are* their Religion. For them, Spirituality is a practical, functional part of everyday life, inseparable from one's personal experience. They sense the spirit in all things— even an animal's prints and the track a bird has left in the sky have a spirit that can be seen and followed. Their language is spiritual expression, as is the way they walk and use Fire and care for their children. They are living Spirituality.

Natural and Supernatural

The distinction between natural (or physical) and supernatural (or spiritual) rests on the dividing line between what we can grasp with our senses and intellect, and what we can't. That line is ill-defined and not commonly accepted, as it differs from individual to individual and swings back and forth within each of us. It is so arbitrary and changeable that from the Greater Perspective it does not exist—there is no physical and spiritual. Everything is natural. For example: Thunder and Lightning are supernatural occurrences until they are understood, mountaintops are the realm of the gods until they are climbed, healings that are miracles to some are within the realm of normal, understood occurrences to others.

This awareness need not detract from the power and mystique of such occurrences. When we know that nothing is beyond our grasp, everything is within the realm of our own personal experience, allowing us to come back and recognize the Supernatural in all things. The mystery contained in a breath is just as profound as that in the Thunderbeings rolling and flashing overhead.

The concept of the spiritual and the physical as separate autonomous entities is likely a fabrication of the out-of-Balance, linear side of the brain— a result of its propensity toward quantifying, isolating, and comparing. The personal inner turmoil and external friction caused by such artificial dichotomizing may be quieted somewhat by positioning the dividing line between the spiritual and physical at a certain point and dogmatically adhering to it. When two or more People agree on the existence and placement of that line, they have left the realm of personal contact with spirit and have begun to practice Religion. Faith and belief then placate the thirst for individual search and personal validation.

Another example of dichotomizing is the anthropologists' yen for categorizing Old Way Peoples as either monotheistic (one god) or polytheistic (many gods), when in actuality they are something beside these two labels that defies categorization. Old Way cosmology incorporates timeflows and interdimensional relationships that take long periods of cultural immersion to grasp; there are no words, much less a single word, to capture that.

The relationship of spirit-entities to each other also finds no direct counterpart: Native People generally know spirits as fingers of a common hand rather than the Civilized tendency toward separate tiers of entities under a master entity.

Some find it hard to accept the nonexistence of a purely supernatural realm because it leaves them on shaky ground with their beliefs in afterlife and supreme being. I was once with She Who Talks With Loons when she was asked by a Civilized Person whether or not she believed in god. She replied that she was an atheist. I think her statement was more to create an attentive audience than to communicate, because it hardly conveyed her awareness. Actually, her concept of spirit is so removed from the Civilized awareness that I think most would consider her an atheist even if she had words to fully convey her concept.

Having Journeyed this far together, we know that, for Native People, concepts of life and spirit, and the language, culture, and lifeway that rest upon them, do not necessarily run a parallel with Civilized concepts. So, the elements of one Way may not find their counterpart in the other. The Supreme Being concept is a potent example.

The purported SkyFathers, Great Spirits, etc., of Old Way Peoples are largely the inventions of missionaries, brought on by their wishful thinking. To think that a people who honor the spirit-life in all things and honor all things as beings on the same par as themselves would have a single spirit predominate over others is a stretch of the imagination. The missionaries take the Native awareness of spirit and the Life-Pulse of the Greater Circle as belief in the Civilized god and supplant the legend-hero with their christ-figure.

And they don't stop there; efforts to entice Natives and usurp the Power of their spirit-way include building churches on sacred sites, overlapping Religious holy days with days of ritual observance, and giving Religious makeovers to traditional ceremonies and customs. Examples from the Christian tradition are Easter and Christmas, and their less successful attempts with Halloween and All Souls Day, which still hold some of their old Power. These (and previously mentioned) transpositions are sometimes subtly and calculatedly executed. At other times—especially when met with cool reception—they can be not-so-subtly force-fed.

Belief and Debwewin

The rain shower was welcome on such a sticky afternoon. Talks With Loons and I sat it out under a shrubby Maple on an outcrop midway through the dense Alder swamp we were picking our way through. Maybe it was the cool, newly scrubbed air that inspired me to do something silly and ask Talks With Loons a question expecting a real answer. I regretted doing it even before I had it completely blurted out, as she had been drawing me to the awareness that answers come as one is ready; questions need not be asked.

On top of that, I asked her a question that was prying and disrespectful, as it was one I should only have been asking of myself. But I didn't trust myself, so in that uncontrolled instant I grasped at the personal findings of someone whose wisdom I did trust. I felt that if I could somehow adopt hers, I would not have to continue my agonizing personal quest.

Even though many years have passed, I feel the blush of shame all over again as I recount this episode. Asking a friend to share his beliefs is acceptable, but with one's Guide it is simply out of line. I fully expected—and deserved—a rebuff, or more likely from Talks With Loons, a respectful and forgiving avoidance of the question, as though she heard nothing.

To my shock, she looked at me with deep face and liquid eyes, which told me she took my request as appropriate and was going to speak. Being quite sure of my respected Guide's reaction, I flushed with conflicting emotions at this unexpected turn. The profound reach of her words added another roiling dimension to my confusion.

I hold those words as perhaps the most moving verbal expression of the guiding substance of one's Path that I have been gifted to hear. As Talks With Loons would wish, I will share her words with you. In Honor of her gift, I will begin on the next page, so that only her words appear:

What is, is.

Debwewin roughly translates as *Truth* in the Ojibway language. Debwewin is what is—what we have each gained as the direct result of our personal awareness, experience, and quest for guidance and unfoldment. Debwewin is our personal reality; it has no application beyond the self.

What exists beyond Debwewin falls in the realm of *Belief*, which various dictionaries define as "acceptance . . . without proof, mental conviction," "acceptance of something as true . . . based on . . . the authority of the source." Beliefs are held not on personal validation, but on *Faith*: "complete, blind acceptance . . . not susceptible to proof," ". . . not supported by reason."

Personal beliefs change in the course of one's life, and there are thousands of religions based on thousands of often conflicting belief systems. If there is only one Spirit-Way (as the bulk of them profess, and the bulk of them hold exclusive claim to), only one of them, in theory, can have a corner on The Way. But there are so many who claim exclusivity, and none of them has yet shown a clear path to The Way, so it may be possible that none of them has it cornered. This may not be a very solid foundation from which to approach spirit, nor upon which to base one's Lifepath.

Belief systems are based on some *person's* interpretation of spirit. These interpretations lead to the continuous and irresolvable debates over whether so-and-so was a virgin or not, which of the scores of names is THE name for the supreme being, whether or not this or that ritual or recitation is THE one the supreme being hears, how many times the Human spirit recycles, and so on. From the Greater Perspective, do these things really matter? Does ascribing to one or the other of these myriad beliefs help make it truth? Does it make any tangible difference in the walking of the Lifepath?

Such are the pillars of the Religions which vie to be wrapped in our fabric of Belief. Charisma, pomp-and-circumstance, and the invoking of divine sanctions are their persuasions that their Path to spirit is better, that Belief is more truth than Debwewin. To accept Belief is to relinquish Personal spiritual Power, to deny the Gift of Vision, and perhaps to forego our unique place in the Circle.

In the Old Way a person is encouraged to seek Debwewin, and a high regard is accorded those who seek it. Purchasing or otherwise ascribing one's personal Debwewin to another is an accepted though not common or esteemed practice.

Some Native cultures have individuals known as Contraries, whose role is somewhat akin to the Civilized Way's satirists and comedians. Nothing is off limits; even the most sacred of Ceremonies is fair game for

Contraries. Their probing satire and oftentimes irreverent antics stimulate questioning and personal validation, which encourages Debwewin over Belief.

Where Spirituality is a living, tangible part of everyday existence and based upon personal experience, Belief and Faith are rare. To paraphrase a saying which speaks it clearly: If a religion doesn't provide or dance or sleep well, leave it be.

Spiritual Exercises

'Chi Debwewin

A couple pages back I shared with you She Who Talks With Loons' personal philosophy—all three words of it. Within that simple, eminently eloquent phrase lies that which transcends the barriers of belief, culture, time, and place. In its purest sense, it knows no division of species or element and applies to all that have spirit. It is the only place in which spirit-communication exists; it is the seat of attunement and the core of Oneness—'Chi Debwewin—the Everywhere Truth.

The Quest for 'Chi Debwewin is for wizened Seekers who have cried through the ethos of their cultural spirituality and the tinting of their own eyes. They have found that doubt is of the mind, and that Truth is found elsewhere. Words and concepts and prayers are to them as a sigh is to the Wind. They hear instead the language of rhythm and flow and cycle. To them, contemplating the like of angels and guardian spirits and sacred places and objects is like attempting to corral a sunbeam from the daylight. Their Seeking has verified that the Circle has no ends, the Lifeflow has no direction or substance to isolate, quantify, or claim.

We who are Journeying together in this book are likely not feathered enough to actively Seek 'Chi Debwewin, for if we were it is improbable that we would be reading this. However, we can draw closer to 'Chi Debwewin by partaking in the practices and absorbing ourselves in the concepts that spring from it. They—the Sweat Lodge, Drum, Fire, Circle, Respect—are visible filaments of the unseen web, universal in their practice and honoring of all spirit.

These things manifest the Everywhere Truth for each of us only if or when they touch us in that place deep below words and thoughts. If they do not, they may not be 'Chi Debwewin, or they may find us in another day and time. The following test brings visibility to the filament of 'Chi Debwewin our Path has presently feathered us for.

Because of what is asked of us in the testing, each test is a Quest in itself. Our tools are the powers of observation, revelation, and direct experience that we have developed thus far. The criteria are stringent; what we wish to test begs verification as Debwewin not only within our realm, but within the realms of other Humans, cultures, and times. Then it needs to be given the same verification by the realms in which dwell the hooved, the rooted, the rocks, and the Wind.

The test is a Ceremony in our growing harmony with the Rhythm of the Spheres. That which passes a test is a glimmer of the knowing that is shared by those of Wisdom; it is a taste of the deep kinship that makes us brothers and sisters of all that is.

In our Seeking, let us keep a perspective on the place of 'Chi Debwewin in our lives: It is the generic and all-touching truth, quite distinct from the very personal truths that we each carry as the Gifts of our Paths.

Prayer

"Grandfathers, this woman has nothing to ask for; she only wishes to give thanks for the Blessings she has been given."

This Sweat Lodge Song by She Who Talks With Loons is perhaps the most pure and beautiful I have been blessed to hear.

The connotations of Prayer as most us know it include supplication, contrition, and the asking of personal favors. Because these practices are irregular and lowly held in the Old Way, I prefer to use the term *Song* when referring to Native Prayer. (The High Prayer of some Civilized traditions also warrants the term.)

Song is living Prayer. When Native People are first given the Civilized idea of there being a time, place, way, and attitude for Prayer, their response is that they do not have to make special arrangements to Pray because their every touch and step and breath is Prayer. Song is the Honor and Respect that is intrinsic to every inner and outer activity as one walks his Path; it is the continuous acknowledgment of spirit in everything. In its essence, Song is being, Song is Balance, Song is Thanksgiving.

"My worship is communion, not grovelling."
—*reaction of Native Person to persistent missionary pressure to join their ritual prayer service.*

If we Walk in Balance, Honor, and Respect, we have little need or thought of begging favor or of guilt. However, when those close to us are in deep pain or stress, we feel the pulling need to implore for their aid.

A Native Person is conservative when asking for something for another, knowing that he is responsible for what he asks. He may be interfering with something that is progressing as intended, or, if his request is granted, he may be asked to provide the energy for its implementation. What he has asked to be given may be gathered from him in some fashion. Because he has initiated the process, he has assumed the burden of outcome and accountability.

With Native People, implorations for the aid of others are an acknowledgment and empowerment of an already ongoing process more so than a request for intervention, so no deficit is accrued. Many of us, new to the Native Way, bring our accustomed credit-deficit ways into our Song. We are not yet aware that, just as with money, we have to pay back that which we spend and do not have to spend.

I am saddened for the People whose Songs ask for something for nothing, because I fear they are running up a debt. Unwittingly, they are robbing the future to empower the moment, and either they or their children will shoulder the burden of debt. I have to suppress the urge to breathe the Old Way into them, so that they will know the moment empowers itself. The old Teacher in me screams release, so that he can open their holy books and give them the remnant of the Beauty Way that survives in their High Prayers in such as, "Father, not my will, but Thine, be done."

Group activities benefit from empowering a sense of shared spirit and giving thanks for everyone's presence and abilities before beginning. This sharing of Song dedicates the task and heightens group recognition to purpose. Sacred undertakings, such as the Hunt, Gardening, and Lodge-building draw their participants into unified directedness and fullness of the moment by first joining their Songs as One. Doing such also draws mealtimes into the Circle of Blessing and reassures those undertaking long trips that they do not travel alone.

In Song, erect posture is respectful and shows alertness and involvement. The lungs function more efficiently and there is less chance of pinched nerves and restricted circulation, which could otherwise interfere with full involvement. As with all that involves attunement, I prefer to have no metal on my body, as the conductive properties of metals could distort subtle energies and rhythms.

Elders
Mircea Eliade, *The Sacred and the Profane*
John Sharkey, *Celtic Mysteries*
Dennis and Barbara Tedlock, *Teachings from the American Earth: Indian Religion and Philosophy*
Christopher Vecsy, *Traditional Ojibwa Religion and its Historical Changes*

Attunement with our Circle is losing our identity to it, being absorbed in its myriad folds and personalities and knowing their emotions and sensations as our own . . .

Circle Attunement

Sun was just beginning to warm the dewy Meadow as I began my Ceremony to the Directions in Thanksgiving for the recent revelation of my Medicine Plant. As I turned to face the Northwest, dimension disappeared. The tall Bluestem Grass directly before me, the Pines at Meadow's edge, the azure Sky beyond, and the space behind my eyes all crashed together and radiated outward. They filled the space with their common presence.

I looked at the Pines; they were still there as my eyes remembered them, yet they were at the same time both transparent and of more substance. Sky was within the Pines, which was within my Cherished One's smile, which was within the blade of Grass before me.

Attunement with our Circle is losing our identity to it, being absorbed in its myriad folds and personalities and knowing their emotions and sensations as our own. You and I have now Journeyed far together; we know much of this depth of Harmony. Now we must learn of its apparent contrary side so that it will not interfere with the Native meditation to Circle Attunement we will be joining in a few steps.

Harmony in Discord

To the Civilized ear, Native song can sound off key and unmelodious, its singers showing little concern for harmonizing. The voices flow according to inner dictates, whereas Civilized song, usually intended for others, is externally governed so that it be harmonious and entertaining.

In the Old Way, there is Harmony in discord; the Great Song of Life is made up of the sundry voices of all of the Kin from the Clans and Kingdoms of the Air, the Rock, the Fire, and the Water. There is no greater, no more lush or resonant, Harmony (which is all the more glorious when we consider the self-absorbed and discordant nature of its individual components).

We consider being in Harmony with other people when we are in a state of peaceful coexistence. This is a surface peace akin to that of a harmonizing chorus; we on this Journey are seeking the deeper peace that has no qualm with the surface discord caused by the interplay and seeming contradictions of all The Great Mother's children seeking their individual Ways.

The deep peace that we are to find lying within this discord cannot be known here on the wake of these words. Rather, we will find it as the coming meditation reveals the Grand Web of Life, which interlaces all that is in an enmeshing, fluid syncopation. This will give us the only peace there is, the everlasting peace that has served Creation from its first glimmerings to the moment before us. Efforts at peace amongst our kind will then reveal themselves as nothing more than feeble and momentary periods of imposed absence of surface violence.

Civilized People cannot know this intrinsic peace because it does not fit their cultural pattern—it cannot be spoken of and intellectually pondered; it cannot be controlled, sold, decreed or moralized. They live in a windowless room trying to create light when there is Light all about them. It's as though they poked out the eyes of their People when they first diverged from the Old Way, for if the Light could still have been seen, no person would have turned from it. (In the two previous chapters we explored to some degree how this occurred, and we explore further in Part III of Book III.)

Those of us who are coming from the Civilized Way have three potential impediments to Circle Attunement, which are listed below so that we can be aware of them and make the effort to keep them from interfering:

— We are accustomed to a consumable, digestible god—quantifiable, intellectually graspable, emotionally and morally aligned.

— We are conditioned to separate the physical and spiritual.

— Because it is superficially the closest in concept and structure to our habitual, learned perspective, we have a tendency to approach spirit from a "high" place and we look for the evolved, ethereal aspects of the Old Way approach. In doing so, we overlook the multitude of enriching, sometimes minute, aspects that give dimension to the matters of everyday life.

Coming to Oneness—a Circle Attunement Exercise

Meditation is experiencing the self beyond ego—beyond feelings and thoughts. By abandoning our conscious identities, we open the potential for communion with that which also exists beyond ego. We do so by entering the unbounded world either within or beyond us.

Turning inward, known as Passive Meditation, is practiced mainly by those of the Civilized Way. For example, Hindu meditation known by the term *Yoga*, roughly translates as, "diverting the senses from the outerworld and becoming absorbed with inner thought". (Meditation is also integral to the practice of Buddhism, but the more recently evolved Islam and Christianity relegated meditation to their ascetics as the religions became closely aligned with state power.)

Turning outward, or Dynamic Meditation, is the form used by most Old Way Peoples. Both forms achieve the same end and are equally effective; lifeway compatibility determines which is practiced.

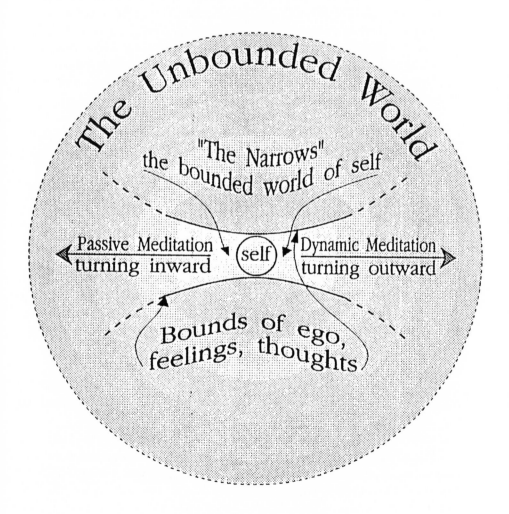

Chart 11. The Self Beyond Self

The big difference between the two forms is in technique. Controlled breathing and chanting are used as aids to Passive Meditation; becoming absorbed in something beyond the self is the Dynamic method. The latter is preferred by most of us on this Journey because the withdrawal of the Passive method can interfere with, and possibly run contrary to, the awarenesses and some of the attunement exercises we use in becoming as one with the Greater Circle.

Once practiced, the meditative state can be entered with less effort and less formal technique. Appropriate music or a quiet moment is all that some Passive Meditators need; Dynamic Meditators may be triggered by walking (see Earthwalker chapter in Book III) or the flight of a bird.

Whatever the technique, successful meditation brings us from a state of Self-Attunement (active body—fast rate of metabolism, senses play a secondary role to rational mind, time awareness) to a state of Circle Attunement (slowed metabolism, enlivened senses, in the now). The Self-Attunement state is required for participation in the Civilized Way, and the state of Circle Attunement is naturally engendered in the Old Way, so Civilized People have more need to consciously meditate, and more need to learn technique.

Some Civilized People, having an innate thirst for Circle Attunement but not knowing how to achieve it, turn to the consumable, readily available consciousness-altering tools of their culture. In doing so they unwittingly short-circuit their potential to develop and experience the bliss of Personal Power and may end up controlled and placated by their ingested "technique." They alter the functioning of their Primary Senses as well, which warps their ability to experience the lushness and full dimension of Attunement, as is intended for them. (More on this in the Alterants chapter in Book II.)

I refer to the Meditative State as *Oneness*. Oftentimes, as I Come into Oneness, I experience an energizing, tingling feeling (which a Yoga practitioner told me she knows as *Shakti*). It begins in the pelvic area near the base of my spine, traveling quickly upward and outward as it radiates throughout my body.

Although not as all-consuming as an orgasm, that's the feeling I could most closely compare with Oneness. It brings me to a state of protracted, enlivening bliss and sensitized awareness, as opposed to post-orgasmic contentedness and mellowness.

A cushion of Moss overlooking the bouldered hillside invited my presence. As I sat there, a gentle breeze washed me of my thoughts and worries. Soon I noticed an Ant picking her way through the Lichen Forest on the Rock at my feet. She met another; they made a brief exchange and continued on their individual ways.

Then I noticed more and more Ants on the Rock, and Ants on neighboring Rocks, all going about activities that took on greater organization and overall purpose as I gained perspective. As my panorama broadened, I saw other colonies, and I imagined many more in the garden of boulders that extended down to the valley.

The hill beyond the valley was also speckled with boulders, and beyond that I could see the treelines of farther hills. I became lost in the vastness of my gaze, absorbed into the myriad of Ants in the innumerable colonies amongst the boulder forests on hills that rolled to the horizon. I came to the hill as a single Ant and left it as a cell of the body that is all Ants, as a wisp of the spirit that flows within all Ants.

The above is a recounting of my first experience in Coming to Oneness. The technique I used works best at first in an expansive natural setting. Once we become accustomed to being in Circle Attunement, the expanse of a leaf may be setting enough, and a glance at that leaf may give time enough. Following is a sequence of steps:

— Choose a place as free of visual and noise pollution as possible, with the potential for the immediate environment to expand into the distance.

— Get comfortable

— Let rational brain clutter pass through, without either suppressing it or giving it energy. Whatever is suppressed will fester and erupt stronger at a later time; whatever is given energy will take on more prominence than its due.

— Focus on something at your feet, using Envisioning (see Sensory Attunement chapter) letting your growing awareness of the object of your attention, with its Greater Circle, carry you into that Circle.

— Gradually switch from Focused to Circle Sight (see Sensory Attunement chapter), letting your growing awareness of the connection of the object of your attention, with its Greater Circle, carry you into that Circle.

— When your identity has lost itself to the Circle, you are in Oneness with it. Remain in your comfortable position if you have Come to Oneness to contemplate, or get up and Walk it into your life. Using it as an end in itself ("for the high") is a trivialization and disrespectful use of a tool intended to draw us into Attunement with our Circle.

A few of us will at first have some trouble either becoming focused on something near at hand or going beyond it. Be resourceful; use anything that works—a fissure in the bark of a Tree, a Cricket's chirp, a Caterpillar noisily chewing a leaf. The important thing is that we not get stuck within the Caterpillar but flow through him and let him carry us beyond ourselves and beyond him like a spreading river delta. In doing so we do not wish to leave him behind; we wish to also encompass that which is beyond him. He is one beautiful voice, but only one of the chorus. Imagine him as being like the taste of the first sweet wild Raspberry that makes us want to look for more. We don't forget that first taste; we carry that experience with us as we multiply and embellish it.

Many Civilized People are more familiar, and therefore comfortable, with symbols and images of the Natural Realm than they are with the Natural Realm itself. Those of us with such a background may not feel trusting enough of that Realm to allow Her to draw us beyond ourselves. We are likely not consciously aware of this, so find ourselves at a loss to explain our frustrated attempts at Oneness.

Although reliance upon symbols will eventually stymie evolution, their initial use could be our only practical transitional catalyst. Once we are able to regularly Come to Oneness, the substitution of a living entity for our symbol will be a much easier matter.

The Circle, the most sacred and universal of symbols, works very well in expanding us through and beyond ourselves because we, and all that is, are Spheres within embracing Spheres. Make one from something at hand, such as a flexible twig, plant stem, or vine, then lay it in front of you or hang it on a branch, and focus on its form. As you become absorbed in the Hoop, let it draw you into and through it, then into the Hoops that progressively spiral outward from you—blossoms, the eye of a Bird, a Cricket's chirp, the cycles of Rain and the seasons.

This exercise is but one of the many ways to Circle Attunement. As we continue this Journey together in the next book, Oneness will more and more come to us without conscious effort as an incidental to our unfolding Path to Balance and Personal Power.

Continuing the Journey

I know you now, as a brother, as a sister. And you know me. I feel honored to have walked this turbulent, glorifying Journey with you. We'll continue on together in a circle of Kinship that the span of our years and the differences in time and place won't break.

Now we know Wind and Squirrel; we know their language. That's all we need. At most we may get stumped on a word of theirs, or twisted on a phrase. Perhaps at such times this book can serve as a dictionary. It may also serve as a journal, holding the story of how together we Walked into the Wind.

Still, at this time of parting some of us fear being alone again, even though we consciously know differently. We are more in number than we seem, but we are scattered like Milkweed seeds to the Prairie Wind. So seeking a Guide or someone to learn and share with could be difficult. If I or my family may be of help in some way, write to me at: Medicine Lodge, Three Lakes, Wisconsin 54562-9333.

> May the Blessing Wind
> be at your back,
> and your Vision
> unfold before you.

Francene Hart '92

—where Wilderness is the classroom,
Ancient Voices are the teachers, knowing self
and Balance are the quests.
The Teaching Drum was founded by Tamarack Song.
Please call or write for the current newsletter/course brochure.
7124 Military Road
Three Lakes, Wisconsin 54562
715-546-2944

Journey to the Ancestral Self
is available as an audiocourse on cassette.

Tamarack brings this book to life in its entirety, his voice walking with the listener through explorations of the Native realm of spirit and self.
Running time: 7½ hours, unabridged; 4 cassettes; $26.00

To order, please send check or money order to:
Station Hill Press
Barrytown, New York 12507
(914) 758-5840

All Credit Card Orders accepted by Toll Free Number
1-800-342-1993
Shipping and handling costs: $3

Index

The index is the web whose strands keep us in touch with topics that span more than one chapter. Some meanings will unfold as we progress through the book; the index will help us to backtrack so that we can easily revisit the steps in that unfoldment. The index is also a quick way to take advantage of the relatedness of all the books.   —*from the text*

The second purpose of this index is to provide material for meditation/contemplation. Some of these words are just mentioned within the context of another topic. Yet the context is important as is the plant that nourishes the bloom.

Many of the legged and winged and rooted are respectfully mentioned here to give them credit for their contribution to this book.

About the Author

When TAMARACK SONG is not out communing with The Mother, it's a pretty sure bet he's either researching, writing, or talking about it. He and his family have a primitive Wigwam camp on a Lakeshore in the Northern Wisconsin Forest. He founded The Teaching Drum Outdoor School, where he and others share the skills and awarenesses of Walking the Sun Trail. With a library of old books on Native Lifeway (which he respectfully calls "Elders") and half a lifetime spent learning from Traditional Peoples, he still gives the greatest credit to the Rooted and Winged and Furred who have come forth to guide him.

About the Artist

FRANCENE HART lives with her husband and son in a Northwoods log home at 6020 Peterson Road, Webster, Wisconsin, 54893. An award-winning watercolorist, she describes her work thusly: "The longer my tenure in the Forest continues, the stronger is my awakening to the sense that the whole of Nature is alive and that a deep interconnection exists between all things. My painting is an expression of this. Living where Deer and Porcupine, Bear and Eagle are part of everyday experience has been the primary source for my spiritual and artistic journey."

About the Graphics Artist

Graphics were executed by TIMM SEVERUD, who lives on a pioneer-era homestead near Winter, Wisconsin. He is a wildcrafter and writer who says he simply plays with computer graphics as a necessary part of his writing. Describing himself as a "non-ritualistic, anarchistic Taoist" he says he helped with this book because he believes that, "With every gift/curse we are given, we are also given the responsibility to share our abilities. Each gift of giving is an act of mending the Sacred Hoop of Life, one fiber at a time. . ."